White-tailed Ptarmigan

White-tailed Ptarmigan

GHOSTS OF THE ALPINE TUNDRA

JOYCE GELLHORN

~

Photography by Joyce Gellhorn and Calvin Whitehall

Published by Johnson Books, a Big Earth Publishing company,
3005 Center Green Drive, Suite 220, Boulder, Colorado 80301.
E-mail: books@bigearthpublishing.com
www.bigearthpublishing.com
1-800-258-5830

Cover and text design by Constance Bollen, cbgraphics

9   8   7   6   5   4   3   2   1

Library of Congress Cataloging-in-Publication Data
Gellhorn, Joyce G.
    White-tailed ptarmigan: ghosts of the alpine tundra / by Joyce Gellhorn; photography
by Joyce Gellhorn and Calvin Whitehall.
        p.   cm.
    Includes bibliographical references and index.
    ISBN 1-55566-397-4
    1. White-tailed ptarmigan. 2. White-tailed ptarmigan—Seasonal variations. I. Title.
    QL696.G285G45   2007
    598.6'33—dc22
                            2006036356

Printed in China

For Clait E. Braun, the premier researcher

of white-tailed ptarmigan in Colorado.

His love for and dedication to these birds

is reflected in all his work.

CONTENTS

ACKNOWLEDGMENTS

*T*his project would have been impossible without generous help from many people. First of all, I wish to thank Dr. Clait Braun for his lifetime work with ptarmigan that has elucidated many of their features. I also wish to thank Clait for many wonderful days in the field, where he patiently answered my many questions and pointed out things I would have never seen without his guidance. In addition, Clait read the entire manuscript and made valuable suggestions and corrections. Other ptarmigan researchers who allowed me to tag along with them and provided a wealth of information include Rick Hoffman, Kathy Martin, Ken Geisen, and Denny Bohon.

Vera Walters provided valuable editing assistance by reading the manuscript at many different stages. Vera and I shared wonderful times in the field both in the summer and in winter, and she suggested the title for this book. The energy and expertise of Cal Whitehall has been invaluable—spotting birds in the field, taking photographs, and reading the manuscript. Cheryl Whitehall provided enthusiasm, critical reviews, and drawings. Madeline Estin and Sallie Greenwood read early versions of the manuscript and kept me on track. Karen Kodner clarified my writing in her careful copyediting. I applaud Constance Bollen for her exquisite book design and layout.

Many people have gone into the field with me during all seasons of the year, and to all I say "thank you" for your enthusiasm and spirit. This venture has been more than following the life history of a very special bird. It has taught me about the unique adaptations that occur in natural ecosystems and the value of preserving lands so nature can flourish. Observing the cycles of white-tailed ptarmigan has given me a greater appreciation for life in all its various forms, and I have gained humility and awe. My belief in the need to set aside lands allowing space for the plants and animals that share this globe with us has been strengthened. This is a concept we all need to embrace.

I wish to thank Norlin Library at the University of Colorado for providing research journals and assistance in searching the literature. Mira Perrizo, publisher of Johnson Books, deserves a special thanks for believing in this book and shepherding it through the process of publication.

Some people climb Colorado's high peaks

"because they are there." Pity these folks!

There exists an infinitely better reason to endure windburn,

strained muscles, blisters, and oxygen deprivation:

catching a glimpse of the elusive white-tailed ptarmigan.

—Alan E. Versaw, *Colorado Breeding Bird Atlas*

An alpine meadow with wildflowers and rocks.

PROLOGUE:
A ROCK BLINKS AT ME

**Whatever peace I know rests in the natural world,
in feeling myself a part of it, even in a small way.**

—May Sarton, *Journal of a Solitude*

*A*bout thirty years ago, I hiked up Sundance Mountain from Trail Ridge Road in Colorado's Rocky Mountain National Park. I started in the alpine tundra above the growth of trees and headed to the summit at 12,486 feet above sea level, traversing fields with diminutive plants and rock-strewn hillsides. In late July ribbons of snow still clung to the high mountain slopes, but the sun warmed my back and the scattered, puffy clouds promised fair weather. Among the green grasses and sedges, the colors of miniature wildflowers invoked an artist's palette: yellow alpine avens; golden dwarf sunflowers; lavender sky pilots; milky bistort; pink and white clovers; and magenta, pink, and yellow-green paintbrushes. Rocks from nearby boulder fields spilled onto the meadow. On the rock surfaces, lichens created colorful mosaics of pale green, chartreuse, brown, gray, black, and bright orange.

I enjoyed the splendor of the high peaks and the play of sun and shadows upon the landscape as I hiked. As I bent down to look at a fuzzy dwarf sunflower, a brown and gray rock a few feet ahead diverted my attention. It seemed to blink. I stopped,

A white-tailed ptarmigan hunkers in the meadow.

looked closer, and slowly inched forward. The rock moved, then stopped and hunkered. What was going on? I sat down to observe the dome-shaped rock more closely, and then I saw the rock blink again. The rock, about half as large as a bowling ball, was mottled in white, brown, and black. Unhurriedly, a neck stretched upward, then a feathered body shook and huddled down, looking again like a round rock.

Finally, I made out a bird that looked at me but did not move. I hardly breathed. After a few moments, the bird rose, walked into a meadow, and pecked at leaves and flowers. It

A ptarmigan stretches its neck.

seemed particularly fond of clover blossoms. As I watched, two, three, finally six "rocks" moved and walked to the lush vegetation. Then the ghostlike birds seemed to vanish, blending into the foliage. I had been hiking in the alpine tundra of Rocky Mountain National Park for more than ten years, yet this was my first sighting of the mysterious, secretive white-tailed ptarmigan.

Ptarmigan blend into their environment during all seasons, because their feathers molt from mottled brown in summer to snowy white in winter. They elusively seem to disappear even after you have spotted one of them. Thus, finding ptarmigan feels like a rare treat, a magical event.

White-tailed ptarmigan belong to the same bird family, Phasianidae, as grouse, quail, and turkeys. All the birds in this family have short, rounded wings and, for the most part, prefer to walk instead of fly. There are three different species of ptarmigan, all living in cold environments. Willow and rock ptarmigan are circumpolar, residing in countries in northern latitudes around the world. The white-tailed ptarmigan is exclusive to North America and

How many ptarmigan are in this picture?

ranges from the mountains of south-central Alaska, southward through western Canada, and along the Rocky Mountains into New Mexico.

While all ptarmigan species in North America have white primary wing feathers in all seasons of the year, white-tailed ptarmigan are the only species of grouse with completely white rectrices (feathers on the tail). Typical of birds that spend most of their time on the ground, the rectrices are short and somewhat hidden. The white primary wing feathers are also hidden except when birds fly or when they preen.

White-tailed ptarmigan are the smallest of all ptarmigan species and the only one found south of Canada. The distribution of white-tailed ptarmigan is not continuous, but rather the birds live in isolated "islands in the sky" that extend above the forest. The birds range as far north as south-central Alaska, the north-central Yukon Territory, and extreme western portions of the Northwest Territories. From here the distribution extends southward along the Coastal Mountains and Vancouver Island of British Columbia, into the Cascade Mountains of Washington to Mount Rainier, and south along the Rocky Mountains through southwestern Alberta to northern New Mexico.

A bird in summer plumage displays its white primary feathers and rectrices.

The species has been successfully introduced to suitable habitats outside its native range including the Sierra Nevada in California, Uinta Mountains in Utah, Pikes Peak in Colorado, and the Pecos Wilderness in New Mexico. They were also released into the Wallowa Mountains in northeastern Oregon, but this transplant was unsuccessful.

White-tailed ptarmigan coexist with willow and rock ptarmigan in Alaska and western Canada. They may breed on the same mountain but not in the same habitat. In summer, willow ptarmigan inhabit tree line areas, arctic valleys, and coastal tundra where vegetation is relatively lush and tall. They like moist areas such as pond edges, streamside thickets, and marshy tundra.

Rock ptarmigan live at higher elevations and latitudes, where their typical habitat is rather dry and supports sparse, low vegetation. In the southern and western parts of their North American range, they also frequent low shrub vegetation, more typical of areas used by willow ptarmigan.

White-tailed ptarmigan are strictly alpine birds. They inhabit the highest peaks and share rocky slopes and high meadows with bighorn sheep, mountain goats, marmots, and pikas. At the northern end of their range, white-tailed ptarmigan breed at elevations ranging from 3,000 to 4,000 feet, while in the southern Rockies of Colorado and New Mexico, they rarely summer below 11,500 feet.

Colorado supports the most extensive distribution of white-tailed ptarmigan in the United States outside of Alaska. An estimate of the breeding population of ptarmigan in Colorado is 35,000 birds. White-tailed ptarmigan prefer habitats with short, cool summers and long, cold winters as found in all major mountain ranges in the southern Rockies.

The scientific name for the white-tailed ptarmigan, *Lagopus leucura*, describes some of its characteristics. The genus name, *Lagopus*, comes from the Greek word for "rabbit or hare-footed," because in winter their feet, covered by short feathers, serve as snowshoes and enable the birds to walk upon snow. The species name, *leucura*, originates from the Latin words *leukos* meaning "white" and *oura* meaning "tail."

Since my first sighting of the elusive white-tailed ptarmigan decades ago, I have become more and more intrigued. The more I learn, the more questions I have. How do they adapt to the frigid temperatures in the alpine zone? How do they endure deep snow six to nine months of the year? When I read that ptarmigan gain weight throughout the winter, I was flabbergasted.

I have examined scientific papers, interviewed researchers who study white-tailed ptarmigan, and participated in ptarmigan surveys. Following scientists in the field has enabled me to observe how biologists ask questions and devise techniques to study these

White-tailed   *Willow*   *Rock*

*Comparison of physical differences and distribution in North America
of three ptarmigan species (males in breeding plumage)*

WHITE-TAILED PTARMIGAN	WILLOW PTARMIGAN	ROCK PTARMIGAN
SPECIES: *Lagopus leucura*	*Lagopus lagopus*	*Lagopus muta*
AVERAGE LENGTH 12–13 inches (30–33 cm)	15–17 inches (38–43 cm)	13–15 inches (33–38 cm)
AVERAGE WINGSPAN 16–17 inches (41–43 cm)	20–23 inches (51–57 cm)	17–20 inches (43–50 cm)
AVERAGE WEIGHT 12.6 ounces (360 grams)	21 ounces (590 grams)	15 ounces (422 grams)
PLUMAGE—(Three seasonal per year) Mottled browns and black in summer, white in winter; tail and wings remain white throughout the year.	Darker summer plumage turns white in winter except for black tail; white primary wing feathers	Blackish-brown summer plumage turns white in winter except for black tail; males have distinctive black eyestripe in winter; white primary wing feathers throughout the year
HABITAT Barren, rocky alpine areas and among willows	Low, dense vegetation at treeline	Rocky tundra
SONG Screams, henlike clucks, soft hoots	Low throaty rumble, cackle	Low growls, croaks, and cackles

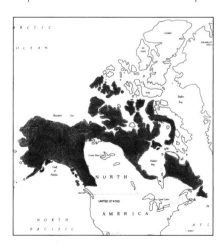

birds. This book records my journeys in learning about white-tailed ptarmigan, whose special adaptations enable them to thrive in the alpine tundra throughout the year. Join me on this month-by-month journey exploring their incredible lives in the highest ecosystem of the Rocky Mountains.

Typical habitat of the white-tailed ptarmigan.

Ptarmigan hen sits quietly, blending in with tundra vegetation.

Willow's surround a subalpine lake—winter ptarmigan habitat.

PTARMIGAN IN THE INDIAN PEAKS WILDERNESS

To stay in one place and watch the seasons come and go is tantamount to constant travel: One is traveling with the earth.

—Marguerite Yourcenar

On a rare windless January morning, the mountains are engraved sharply against the deep cerulean sky, and wind patterns are etched on the cold snow. It's a perfect day for cross-country skiing with my friend Maddie in Colorado's Front Range, located west and northwest of Denver.

Our skis slid smoothly as we climbed through the subalpine forest toward a lake at 11,000 feet. Avoiding the lake's icy surface, we skied around the north side amid large limber pines and Engelmann spruce. Tracks of snowshoe hare, long-tailed weasel, chickaree or pine squirrel, and coyote told stories of life in this frosty environment. Prints of a weasel in an open, sunlit area looped around the base of every shrub. The weasel must have skipped and danced among the sparkling ice crystals just a few hours earlier.

We continued around the lake's western edge, where willows poked above the snow. Our skis sank deeply when air pockets around the bushes subsided. I pointed out some faint windblown tracks to Maddie. The tracks, probably made the day before, made us more alert for signs of animal activity. We skied on, scanning the snow, the willows, and the areas surrounding the timberline trees.

Stopping for lunch, my friend and I relished the sun's warmth, the stillness, and the twinkle of diamonds on the wind-fluted snow. We reluctantly turned downward to the trail-head and skied back on the south side of the frozen lake amid more willows.

Then we saw them—fresh tracks, looking like three small, outstretched fingers pointing forward, punctuating the snow from one willow shrub to the next. I stopped, looked at the snow surface, and skied forward ten feet—stopping again and searching, searching. Finally, I spotted one—a bird white as the snow sat perfectly still at the base of a willow bush. It was totally white except for its black beak and black, beadlike eyes.

I stared at the bird and it stared back at me. I pointed out the bird to my friend. Just then Maddie saw another one huddled at the base of an adjacent bush. We scrutinized the landscape of snowdrifts and willows. Quietly, slowly, we followed tracks to the edge of a

Ptarmigan tracks.

A ptarmigan hides amid willow bushes.

small bank. There, in a protected nook, five more ptarmigan crowded together. The little balls with pure-white feathers barely moved as we approached. They watched us warily. Turning so we could see better under the bank, we discovered two more birds.

A bird closer to us, which we had overlooked, moved slowly toward the comfort of its companions. Then we noticed two more birds almost hidden in a snowdrift. Watching closely, we saw a bird shake itself, wriggling like a belly dancer as it settled deeper into the snow. Altogether, twelve ptarmigan sat on the snow, seemingly oblivious to winter's cold.

The birds' almost regal appearance comes from their puffed-up feathers, which trap air. The air pockets act as a barrier that provides ptarmigan with an added insulating layer. Standing or hunkering in the snow, the stoic ptarmigan appeared as rotund balls etched with soft feathers.

The bird's camouflage worked so well that had we been concentrating more on our skiing and less on scanning each willow as we passed, we would have completely missed seeing this amazing spectacle. Enriched, we thanked the birds for making our outing memorable.

The following day, wanting to photograph these interesting birds, I returned to the Indian Peaks Wilderness. No fresh tracks were visible when I approached the spot where we had seen birds the day before. Nevertheless, I felt confident that they were nearby. I skied a few yards, stopped, scoured the landscape, and continued forward. Suddenly, in my peripheral vision, a half-dozen white birds flew out from the base of the trees at the forest edge. They settled down about twenty yards ahead while other birds slowly walked toward their companions. I stopped to eat lunch, allowing time for the ptarmigan to become accustomed to me.

While I ate, some ptarmigan came out of the trees and headed for the willows, clipping and eating willow buds as they walked. Other birds continued to roost in depressions under some of the larger spruce trees.

A raven circled over the lake, landed on top of a spruce tree above the roosting ptarmigan, and then called as if to say, "This is my territory." Movement of ptarmigan ceased, and I could not spot any of them. I looked with binoculars at the base of the larger

Ptarmigan puff up their feathers in winter to add an insulating layer.

Willow buds make up over 90 percent of a ptarmigan's winter diet.

trees where the ptarmigan had now disappeared. In the middle of the willows were several lumps of snow, but I could see no birds.

Only the raven's call interrupted the tranquil scene. Finally, the raven flew away. Moments later the lumps of snow in the willows started to move. Soon ptarmigan began to feed again. Quietly I crept closer to observe and photograph these imposing birds in their white-feathered robes.

In winter, white-tailed ptarmigan seek out willow areas for their home. They use the snow for protection, digging into it to make snug overnight roosts. Over 90 percent of their winter diet consists of willow buds. By keeping their energy requirements to a minimum, these birds survive in areas where other birds cannot. Living in some of the most hostile environments on earth, white-tailed ptarmigan exhibit great tenacity and beauty!

Signs to look for when conducting the survey: tracks.

SURVEYING FOR PTARMIGAN
ON GUANELLA PASS

Following the signs of wild creatures is an exercise of memory, imagination, and observation, an unending process that leads the tracker farther and farther from himself, into the secret lives of beings that move almost silently, often in darkness, flowing through the spaces we leave vacant. For all our pursuit of them, they remain inscrutable, indifferent to our will. The only way to approach understanding is on their terms, by honing our careless senses down to an almost forgotten edge, by becoming quiet and watchful again, mindful of the wind, always listening, pausing often.

—Nick Jans, *Tracks of the Unseen*

*I*t seemed I had slept only a few hours when my alarm awakened me at 5 A.M., but getting up early was necessary to participate in a ptarmigan survey on Guanella Pass. The pass, located about fifty miles west of Denver, Colorado, is on the Continental Divide at 11,669 feet. I drove to Georgetown, where our group assembled at a small restaurant. There were biologists from the U.S. Forest Service and the Colorado Division of Wildlife, along with volunteers from the Rocky Mountain Bird

Signs to look for when conducting the survey: form and scat.

Observatory and the U.S. Fish and Wildlife Service. Rick Hoffman, a tall, lean researcher with the Colorado Division of Wildlife, explained how the survey would be conducted.

"The area around Guanella Pass attracts the largest wintering population of white-tailed ptarmigan that we know in Colorado," he told us. "Birds gather in large flocks during winter, making this an ideal time to survey their numbers. The persistent snow cover and expanse of willows around Guanella Pass is key to their survival and we are concerned that improving the road over the pass and the trail to Mount Bierstadt will have a negative impact upon the birds.

"To find ptarmigan you need to develop a search image," he continued. "The birds will be hunkered down next to willow shrubs or in a snow roost. Often they sit to the lee side of krummholz trees just at treelimit. Look for disturbances in the snow such as tracks or wing marks, depressions where birds have spent the night, or droppings that look like slightly curved one-inch rods of compressed wood."

We carpooled to the top of Guanella Pass and divided into four groups of six to eight people. Each group was to survey one sector in the three-square-mile study area. Our leader, Denny Bohon, a U.S. Forest Service researcher, distributed GPS units, notepads and pencils, and walkie-talkies to members of our group. She then instructed us to form a line across the sector, spacing ourselves twenty yards apart. Whenever we found sign of ptarmigan such as footprints, scat, or hollowed snow roosts, we called to the GPS person to mark the position, while another person recorded the sign on a notepad.

The range of terrain included windswept open tundra, knoll tops, small bowls, and extensive acres of willow stands. All morning we snowshoed, searching and searching

Scenic view of Guanella Pass, showing extensive willow areas.

without seeing any birds. We saw a few sign of bird activity, but nothing was fresh. On the exposed tundra, the compacted snow was hard, windswept, and fluted by recent gale-force winds. We sighted other animal sign—prints of coyotes, white-tailed jack rabbit, long-tailed weasels, even pug marks of a bobcat. We studied each print to learn which direction the animal was moving and noted other clues of its activity. As we came over a rise, a large jack rabbit bounded away from us. Its white coat would have made it invisible had the animal not moved. Only the brown markings on the tips of its ears showed up in this white-upon-white world. The rabbit bounded rapidly, took a couple of long leaps using all four feet, then stood up and hopped on its large hind feet as it sprinted away.

At the end of the second sweep of our sector, we stopped to regroup: we ate lunch and discussed how to continue. 'This afternoon, we'll drop toward the willows and the creek drainage where there is less wind and the snow will be softer," said Denny. "Try to keep twenty yards apart and call if you see any sign of birds. Remember, if you spot one bird, there is a 99 percent chance you will find others. At this time of year, the birds are very gregarious."

It was much slower going in the soft snow, and we often sank thigh-high even with snowshoes. I was grateful for ski poles to help me get up when I fell. Plodding, plodding, plodding—I almost lost track of time. Will this ever end, I wondered? What had started as an adventure seemed to go on forever without success. Then, Cal Whitehall, my friend and fellow photographer, who was in the survey line twenty yards below me, spotted some tracks verging off at a right angle.

We turned, following the tracks uphill. Tracks became more numerous where birds had stopped at a willow bush to eat a few buds. We had trouble following the tracks on the harder, windswept snow between willow patches because tracks had not penetrated. The bird's toenails only made faint scratches in the surface.

Suddenly the tracks disappeared. Cal pointed out short parallel lines on either side of the last set of marks. "What's that?" he asked.

Ptarmigan tracks ending with wing prints.

In soft snow, ptarmigan shake and settle into the hollow's to roost.

"This is where they flew away," I answered. "Those marks are from their wingtips pressing against the snow as they took off."

"Will they fly far?" Cal asked.

"Usually they fly less than 100 yards as ptarmigan conserve energy by walking instead of flying," I replied.

We concentrated as we continued to search, knowing the birds were probably close by, but for the next twenty minutes we saw nothing.

"Birds!" a shrill voice called out. Someone started to count them: "One, two, four—oh my, there are lots and lots of them." Our yelling did not seem to disturb the birds. They huddled close to the willow shrubs. It almost seemed that the ptarmigan "knew" they were invisible because their white coats blended into the snowy environment.

We gathered around the birds to get the most accurate count possible. Since the birds were on the edge of our sector, people from an adjacent sector helped us encircle the flock. As long as we stayed at least eight to ten feet from the birds, they seemed undisturbed by our presence. While people tried to get a count, the birds pecked at willow buds or sat quietly.

In winter ptarmigan have feathers on their legs and feet, and long, sharp toenails.

Some birds, with puffed-up feathers, pecked at the snow or dug with their long toenails to make a depression in which to roost. Others, in softer snow, wiggled around to make a hollow. Ptarmigan use the snow as an insulating blanket to protect themselves from the harsh wind and cold air.

We counted seventy-two birds in the flock. "About 80 percent of these birds are females or young of the year," Rick Hoffman told us. "Male ptarmigan form smaller flocks and remain higher on mountain slopes than females."

Another researcher added some interesting facts: "Ptarmigan are efficient at keeping warm with a thick layer of fuzzy down feathers under their contour feathers. In addition, their feather shafts are hollow and filled with air. Air is a good insulator, so the hollow feather shafts, along with the dead air spaces between feathers, increases a ptarmigan's insulation."

Another researcher said, "Feathers on their legs act like leggings. Ptarmigan even have feathers on their feet, which, like snowshoes, allow them to walk on soft snow. Feathers on their feet fold out of the way as the birds pick up and bring their feet forward, then flatten on the downstroke to increase their bearing surface."

"Ptarmigan grow dense feathers around their nostrils and even on their eyelids to prevent blowing snow and cold wind from entering and chilling their body," someone added. "Some ptarmigan even have a darker patch behind their eyes that might help to protect their eyes like sunglasses."

As I listened to all the attributes of the ptarmigan's adaptation to winter, I wished I could be a ptarmigan myself with built-in sunglasses and a feathered coat to fluff up and keep me warm. Ptarmigan are certainly more attuned to their winter environment than people, I thought.

Before we left the flock of birds, we checked the ptarmigan's location with a GPS. Finally we finished surveying our sector and returned to our vehicles. It was 4:30 P.M. and I was exhausted. It had been a long day.

A bird exhibits a darker patch of feathers behind its eye.

In Georgetown over steaming cups of coffee and cocoa, we recounted our adventures and assembled data collected by the different groups. Hastily penciled notes, made on small notepads in the field, were transferred to organized data sheets. Rick Hoffman thanked the volunteers. "Counting the number of ptarmigan gives us an estimate of their population, which, when done over a period of years, is a useful tool in showing trends and health of their habitat. Determining whether the population is growing, stable, or declining helps us make management decisions. Besides," he added, "what a great way to spend a beautiful, wintry Saturday!"

A ptarmigan digs a snow roost.

PTARMIGAN
ON MY BIRTHDAY

The stormy March has come at last,
With winds and clouds and changing skies;
I hear the rushing of the blast
That through the snowy valley flies.

—William Cullen Bryant, *"The Snowstorm"*

*M*arch heralds spring at lower elevations, but in the alpine tundra cold and snow still clasp the land. Winds are generally moderate compared to January's fearful blasts, but March is a changeable month and the weather may range from warm, calm, sunny days to heavy snows.

One warm day in mid-March, I counted sixty-two ptarmigan near the summit of Guanella Pass. The birds, undisturbed by my presence, continued their activities of eating, loafing, and digging roosts in the snow as I photographed them. The melted and refrozen surface on the snow created a crust, which some birds pecked at and scratched through to reach softer snow beneath. I watched a bird tunnel in the softer layer until it disappeared from my view.

Other birds fluffed up their feathers and settled in, closing their eyes for a siesta. Occasionally they blinked, opened their eyes to check out their companions, and returned to their slumber. It felt like a lazy day, and I enjoyed sharing the alpine with the ptarmigan.

Another day, I had a very different experience. The wind howled, whirlwinds of snow cascaded down alpine ridges, and it seemed unlikely that we would locate any birds. However, our group persevered. We snowshoed through the willow bushes with the vague hope of spotting some birds. The soft snow often collapsed, and we would sink down. Our slow progress was frustrating, but then we spotted some dimples in the snow—snow roosts where ptarmigan had spent the night!

We continued, and suddenly a bird hidden in the willows became visible. One head popped out of the snow, and another, and another. Completely covered by the blanket of

Heads of ptarmigan pop out from their snow roost.

Even the beak is covered by snow.

snow, the birds only revealed themselves when we came too close to their roosts. The birds looked around and soon disappeared back into their protective white blanket.

One March, a record-breaking snow fell on the first two days of spring. I had never seen so much snow fall at one time: more than 54 inches at my home, at 7,000 feet, and nearly 100 inches at Bear Lake, at 9,500 feet in Rocky Mountain National Park. White covered the landscape, softening shapes of homes, cars, roadways, and trees. I enjoyed seeing how the wild weather controlled everyone's activities. The grand and dramatic storm humbled us and reminded us of the power of nature.

Each day after the storm, I explored a different place in the mountains to see the changes the snow had wrought. On March 30, my birthday, I decided it was time to visit the Indian Peaks Wilderness to see if I could locate "my ptarmigan."

From the parking lot I skied on snow that sparkled like sequins in the morning light. By the time I got to the ptarmigan's wintering area, it was very windy and cold. This was not a good sign, because birds often stay in snow roosts during such severe conditions.

Wind blows newly fallen snow into intricate patterns.

Stopping briefly to put on my balaclava, goggles, and a parka with a warm, protective hood, I headed out toward an area across the lake where I had seen ptarmigan most often that winter.

I stopped frequently to scan the terrain, but I saw no birds. Deep snow covered the willows along the south and west sides of the lake, clearly an ominous sign. Then I asked myself, "If I were a ptarmigan and most of my food source was covered by snow, what would I do?"

Calm after the storm.

Tracks lead to willows from overnight forms.

Answering my own question, I figured the ptarmigan might go to the outlet stream where taller willows grew in a swampy area. There, the willows might still be peeking out above the snowpack. Sure enough, around the outlet stream I found faint tracks that looked as if they had been made the previous day. I scouted the area, looked carefully at the softest snow, and started to ski across a nearby meadow. Then a couple of birds flew directly in front of me, popping out of the snow like popcorn.

They flew ten yards and settled down by the willows poking above the snowpack. Delighted, I spent twenty minutes quietly taking photographs and watching the winter-white birds. The ptarmigan, accustomed to me, unhurriedly ate some willow buds, then scratched at the snow surface to submerge themselves into the drifts. I found more tracks, but soon left the area not wanting to put undue stress on the birds. Seeing my friends fulfilled my birthday wishes, and I bid the ptarmigan a good day.

Male bird with red-orange eye comb.

~April~
LONGER DAYS
INITIATE CHANGES

In a way winter is the real spring, the time when the inner thing happens, the resurge of nature.

—Edna O'Brien, *Mrs. Reinhardt*

*T*he longer days of spring signify a time of renewal for flowers, insects, birds, and mammals. Often, it is a critical transition requiring that animals accumulate enough energy for reproduction. But for white-tailed ptarmigan living high in the mountains, snow depth, temperatures, and wind characterize April as a winter month. So, to get the complete picture of ptarmigan activities in winter, I went on another ptarmigan survey on April 2.

As in previous surveys, a group of volunteers and researchers met in Georgetown for breakfast and attended a brief orientation by Rick Hoffman of the Colorado Division of Wildlife. Some people had been at each previous survey, while some were new. We carpooled to the top of Guanella Pass, divided into groups to cover the different sectors, and used the same methods of making a line of people to look for the birds.

Rick Hoffman and his mentor, Clait Braun, a retired Colorado Division of Wildlife researcher, have surveyed Guanella Pass for over thirty-five years. Often 100 to 150 birds

TIMING OF SEASONAL MOVEMENTS AND ACTIVITIES OF WHITE-TAILED PTARMIGAN

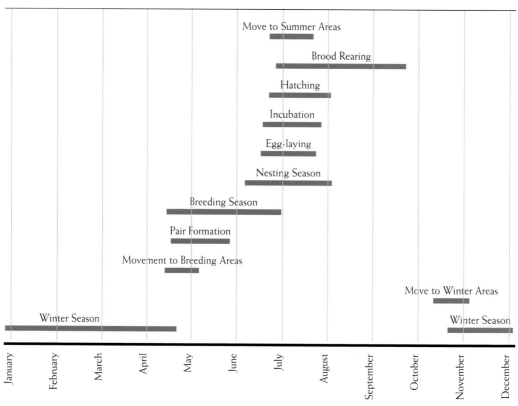

ACTIVITY	APPROXIMATE TIMING
Winter Season	Late October to late April
Movement to Winter Areas	Late October to mid-November
Movement to Breeding Areas	Mid-April to early May
Pair Formation	Mid-April to mid-May
Breeding Season	Mid-April to early July
Nesting Season	Early June to early August (includes renesting activities)
Egg-laying	Early June to mid-July
Incubation	Mid-June to mid-July
Hatching	Late June to early August
Brood Rearing Season	Late June to late September
Movement to Summer Areas	Late June to mid-July

can be viewed on a good day, and studies indicate that between 200 and 250 birds use this area each winter. Birders from around the world frequently visit Guanella Pass to add white-tailed ptarmigan to their life list.

In the life cycle of white-tailed ptarmigan, the timing of the seasons differs from species living at lower elevations. Scientists use the following demarcations:

- **Winter, October 20 to April 30:** At high elevations the snowy season is much longer than our usual concept of winter. The plumage of ptarmigan is winter-white.
- **Spring, May 1 to June 30:** Spring is a short period of unstable weather. Snowy days are interspersed with melting of the snowpack and the first blooming of wildflowers. During this time, ptarmigan molt, establish territories, and mate.
- **Summer, July 1 to August 31:** A brief summer encompasses a flurry of activity, with flowers blooming and setting seed. Ptarmigan nest and raise chicks.

As winter wanes, ptarmigan exhibit signs of pair bonding.

- **Fall, September 1 to October 19:** Early snowfalls mark the end of summer. The shorter days provide a signal for ptarmigan to molt to winter plumage.

Even though researchers consider April a winter month for ptarmigan, we witnessed the first signs of obvious sexual behavior of a pair near some krummholz during our early April survey. The male strutted and displayed his red-orange eye comb to a female who sat quietly, seemingly admiring her suitor. Except for the colorful stripe above the male's eye, both birds appeared almost completely white. Changes were starting, however, and a few darker feathers were noticeable beneath white feathers and around the eyes of some males.

On another visit to Guanella Pass in mid-April, I saw fewer birds, but all showed prenuptial behavior. Males, still mostly white in plumage, displayed red-orange eye combs to the pure white females crouched nearby. By the last half of the month, ptarmigan leave wintering grounds, migrating upward to their breeding territories.

Individuals vary in their timing of life cycle events. The spring molt in males doesn't usually start until mid- to late April, but occasionally a bird begins this process earlier, as seen in 2005 in the Indian Peaks Wilderness Area. One bird had already started its spring molt by March 31, while other members of the flock were still mostly white. At the other extreme, researchers Clait Braun and Kathy Martin reported two female ptarmigan that failed to molt their winter-white plumage. While these birds survived through the summer without their mottled-brown cryptic coloration, it appears they did not breed successfully.

While it seems improbable than any animal can gain weight through the snowiest time of year, male ptarmigan become heavier from September to early April, peaking just prior to establishing territories. Females reach their annual peak a month later, coinciding with nesting and egg laying. During winter, ptarmigan eat nutritious willow buds, rich in proteins, and they roost to minimize their energy expenditure. Like stay-at-home couch potatoes, the birds increase their weight in the coldest season.

One bird starts to molt earlier than usual.

Spring is near.

As the days lengthen in April, hormones in the pituitary and thyroid glands of ptarmigan become stimulated to trigger molting. Males begin the process earlier than females. By the end of April most males will have some barred, tan-and-black feathers along the top of their heads, around their eyes, and on their backs. Because the molt usually progresses from the top of the head downward, males often appear to have hoods.

The changes in ptarmigan's plumage coincides with their upward movement to summer territories. This isn't a continuous transition; birds move higher on pleasant days and retreat downward when late snows blow in. As the weather fluctuates during this late winter and early spring period, birds follow the daily whims of weather conditions. However, all signs indicate changes lie ahead. Winter winds diminish, snow starts to melt, and birds become restless to establish territories and form pair bonds.

A male ptarmigan defends his territory from May through July.

PTARMIGAN MOLT
AND ESTABLISH TERRITORIES

Observing this champion of camouflage that changes from pure white to a mottled gray-brown-black-white in summer is one of the special joys of tundra walking. For Clait Braun . . . observing ptarmigan is not only a joy, it's practically a way of life.

—Ruth Carol Cushman, *"On the Ptrail of the Ptarmigan"*

A number of years ago in early May 1995, with an almost complete snowpack on mountain peaks, I snowshoed on Guanella Pass and searched in vain for white-tailed ptarmigan. I scanned for white or mottled birds among the willows of the ptarmigan's wintering grounds, but saw nothing. I walked to a hollow filled with bushes and up another slope, stopping to scrutinize the landscape. Fuzzy pussy willows poked above the three-foot-deep snowpack, evidence of the season's changes. Signs of ptarmigan abounded. Clipped buds and branch tips marked where they had eaten, and their scat in snow hollows revealed roosting forms, but I saw no birds. Perhaps the birds had already migrated upward to breeding territories as they often do in late April and the beginning of May. I had thought the heavier-than-usual snowpack would

A female in mid-May starts her spring molt later than male birds.

delay their migration, but no birds were visible. Later I read a report by researcher Terry May, who found wintering areas were devoid of ptarmigan by April 20 each year. In the Indian Peaks Wilderness, as well, I never found flocks in wintering areas after mid-April.

Males fly one to five miles from their wintering areas, located at timberline or in bowls in the lower alpine, to higher slopes to reach their breeding territories. Each bird looks over the landscape and selects a suitable spot with rocks, willow shrubs, and moist alpine vegetation. Often a stream is nearby. Mature males typically return to the same territory year after year.

Snows may pile deeply during spring, forcing ptarmigan to first occupy sites close to the upper limit of krummholz trees and later to enlarge their territories as the snow melts. Small patches of willows among tree islands sustain the birds until the herbaceous vegetation greens up.

Soon after a male ptarmigan selects a living space, he advertises his acquisition with calls of ownership. In mid-May 1989, as I was coming down Flattop Mountain toward the upper reaches of treelimit, I heard a bird call. The sound varied between a louder "khir-khir" and a softer cooing. I walked around a small tree island toward the sound and saw a male ptarmigan strutting, flashing his red-orange eye comb. Breeding season was approaching, and the color of the flamboyant patch above the male's eye had intensified.

The bird's speckled head and neck contrasted with his white body. He walked back and forth with such purpose that I felt certain another bird must be nearby. I wondered whether the cock was defending his territory from another male or if he was courting.

After ten minutes, I finally spotted the source of the ptarmigan's actions—a nearly pure-white female huddled under a bush. She seemed to be hiding, perhaps because she had barely started to molt and had just arrived on the breeding territory. Shortly after I spotted her, the ptarmigan hen walked over to a snowpatch and hid among the willows. Ptarmigan seem aware of their coloration and often seek that part of their environment that matches their own color.

During the third week of May 2005, I snowshoed up Mount Ida in Rocky Mountain National Park and watched and listened as white-crowned sparrows, perched on top of

A male ptarmigan on Mount Ida.

Dryas leaves become green along the edges of melting snow.

willows and flagged timberline trees, sang flutelike breeding trills. Even in areas of copious snow, springtime warmth filled the air and breeding birds responded.

Going upward, I scanned the scenery for other signs of spring. Insects—snow fleas, mosquitoes, crane flies, and ladybugs and other beetles—dotted snowfields. Flocks of rosy finches and American pipits swooped down to glean the abundance. The intense sun melted the snow's surface and water percolated through the snowpack. Often my snowshoes sank deeply along the drift edges. A few small green leaves and new sprouts appeared among dried vegetation on the water-soaked ground between drifts.

I trudged upward to a windswept tundra ridge that offered vistas of Specimen Mountain and the Never Summer Range. What spectacular views! Soon, building cumulus clouds turned dark gray, and I heard thunder in the distance. It was time for me to turn down and go back toward timberline. A need for a short rest made me head for a spot of dry ground where I put down my pack and sat upon hummocks of dried grasses. I took a water bottle out of my pack and scrutinized the edges of the snow—and then I saw him. Hunkered down not twenty feet from me was a male ptarmigan. He was silent, just sitting, and almost invisible at the interface between the tan ground and the white snow. I recognized the bird as a male by the bars of black and brown feathers interspersed with white ones on his chest—a sign of his nuptial plumage. I sat quietly to observe and take some photographs. The cock ptarmigan ignored me at first, and then he slowly walked away. Later, looking at the vegetation greening at the edge of the drift, I recognized green dryas leaves, a new food source for the ptarmigan as he established his territory.

Much of what we know about the population dynamics and behavior of white-tailed ptarmigan is the result of Clait Braun's research with the Colorado Division of Wildlife. Clait has studied ptarmigan for forty years, beginning when he was a graduate student at Colorado State University. At that time, little was known about these alpine birds. Some of the questions that Clait wished to explore included:

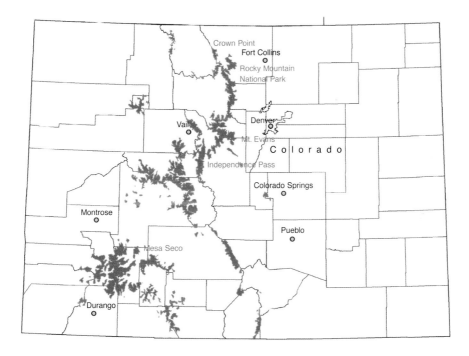

Map of ptarmigan range in Colorado and Clait Braun's field sites (in blue).

- How long do white-tailed ptarmigan live? What is the age structure of birds in a population?
- What is the area of white-tailed ptarmigan territories? Do birds use their same territories year after year and pair with the same mates?
- What do white-tailed ptarmigan eat at different seasons of the year? How can they survive living in the alpine tundra during winter?

At first, even finding birds was a challenge. White-tailed ptarmigan live in seldom-visited areas, and sightings of the birds were spotty. In 1966, the first summer of his study, Clait hiked for miles and miles in alpine areas to determine suitable study locations. He scanned the surroundings and listened for calling birds. Although sometimes he didn't see ptarmigan, he classified an area as being occupied if he heard the birds' calls or saw droppings or feathers.

By taping the various sounds of ptarmigan, Clait started to recognize different patterns. In springtime, males utter a distinctive, territorial-challenge call. Clait played these taped

Clait Braun snares a bird.

calls in his study sites during the next field season, and as a result he found more birds and began to observe their behavior. As males established territories, Clait followed them to plot the birds' home range. Eventually, he mapped twenty-six territories in a two-square-mile area along Trail Ridge Road in Rocky Mountain National Park. Other study sites were at Crown Mountain in the Roosevelt National Forest, Mount Evans, Independence Pass, and Mesa Seco in the San Juan Mountains.

Clait's passion for research on white-tailed ptarmigan increased as he became more and more involved in working with the birds. He loved being in the alpine during all seasons of the year, and the more he learned, the more questions he asked.

Clait needed to identify individual birds to accurately observe interactions between them. He modified a type of fishing pole he had used in a grouse study. The pole could be extended up to twenty-two feet, and its end was fitted with a loop of nylon fishing line to snare birds. Clait edged the pole with the noose just in front of a ptarmigan. The bird, not seeing the clear fishing line, often walked right into the noose, which Clait quickly

The bird flies, trying to escape the noose.

retracted. Grabbing the snared bird, Clait took off the noose and placed the bird into a cotton sack. While snaring birds in this fashion startles them, it does no harm, and a frightened bird placed in a cotton sack soon becomes calm. Quickly, Clait weighed each bird by attaching the string closing the sack to a spring balance. Gently, Clait took the bird out of the sack and held it as he made observations and took measurements. He noted the bird's sex, size (the length from beak to the end of the tail), molting condition, color of the feathers, the size of the eye comb, and the condition of the feet and toenails. He held the bird firmly, and stroked it and talked to it in a low voice, which seemed to calm even the most excited bird.

Next he placed bands on the bird's legs. Clait rested the bird's back against his chest, holding the bird's legs outward. In addition to standard bands used by the Division of Wildlife, each ptarmigan was marked with a combination of different-colored plastic bands. For example, a mature male bird might have a white band above a green band on its left leg and a white band above a blue band on its right leg, which would be notated

A bird is banded so it can be identified in the future.

(from left to right) as "W/G W/Bl." This method of banding birds enabled researchers to identify individual birds year after year. Some individuals have been followed for as long as twelve years.

Now that they had the ability to identify individual birds, Clait and other researchers recognized that male ptarmigan returned to the same territories year after year. When the male arrives, he often sits upon a prominent rock and gives a territorial call. This call attracts females and warns other males to stay away. The cock defends his home range with great theatrical displays: flying into the air, calling, gliding downward, and then sitting again upon the rock to vocalize. When another male intrudes, the territorial bird will strut and shriek. This is followed by a standoff, each bird standing erect with his tail cocked, screeching ownership until one concedes.

Not all males are successful in finding a suitable territory. Most yearlings return to areas near where they were born, but few find available space; they remain along the edges of established breeding grounds and do not mate. Sometimes they are able to secure a site by filling a territory vacated by a male that has not returned. Most males travel only short distances from their wintering grounds to territories near their birthplace.

Female ptarmigan travel farther to seek mates on mountains away from their natal territory—a practice important in maintaining genetic diversity within a population. They migrate either singly or in small groups and move as far as twenty to thirty miles from their winter habitat. Arriving at a breeding territory, hens may still be mostly white or have only a few brown or gray feathers. Shortly, mottled black, tan, and yellow feathers replace the white feathers. Although females begin to molt two or more weeks later than males, they molt faster. By the first week in June, they are almost impossible to spot among the tundra rocks.

As a ptarmigan hen examines potential mates, she appears to check out the quality of a male's territory as well as his attractiveness. When she finds a suitable partner, she moves in. Some hens seem more fickle than others. Yearling females may start courtship activities with one male, only to move to another mountain ten to fifteen miles away to breed and raise a family.

Clait and Joyce in the field.

A male ptarmigan sits on a prominent rock to advertise his territory.

Ptarmigan commonly form lifetime bonds with their mates even though they stay together on a territory for only two to three months each year. The common name *ptarmigan* was given to this genus by Eskimos, for the word means "humanlike," and it describes the birds' faithful nature in pairing up year after year. As with people, some ptarmigan are more faithful to their partners than others. Occasionally a male mates with two hens on adjacent territories. The proportion of polygamous males varies annually and is related to over-winter survival. For example, if more males die during the winter, polygamy seems to increase.

Although many ptarmigan form stable pair bonds year after year as long as both partners are alive, the practice of marking individuals has shown that some birds switch mates. For example, one female successfully mated with the same male for three years, then

Alpine flowers that ptarmigan eat in May and June: Forget-me-nots.

switched and mated with a male on an adjacent territory. In her fifth breeding season, however, she switched back and paired with her original partner.

Ptarmigan can form pairs as early as mid-April, but late-spring snowstorms reverse reproductive activities. Hens will move downhill to willow basins below timberline, and males congregate in small flocks adjacent to breeding areas. Then as the weather moderates, birds again move upward to their territories. Thus, the period of courtship and breeding varies from year to year depending upon climatic conditions.

Breeding usually occurs at the same time as the blooming of the first alpine flowers—sky-blue forget-me-nots, yellow snow buttercups, and lavender pasque flowers. Ptarmigan diversify their diet as herbaceous vegetation becomes green and flowers begin to bloom. In addition, they also feast upon insects found on snowfields and between developing plants.

As days become longer and the snow melts, ptarmigan begin to establish territories and form pairs. Changes in weather modify the birds' behavior: they may be forced downhill in a snowstorm, or allowed to migrate upward when a storm clears. Finding birds during this changeable season is often frustrating, since the birds no longer occupy winter habitats but their breeding territories are not yet firmly established.

Snow buttercups.

Dwarf clover.

Spring beauty.

Clait Braun has more success at finding birds during this unstable season than I because he plays recorded territorial calls. Recently on Mount Evans in mid-May, we listened for birds to respond to the played recordings. As Clait located birds, he noosed them, took measurements, banded unbanded birds, and assessed how many territories were located within a particular area. Birds were most active between 5:30 and 9:30 A.M. On warm, sunny days, their activity decreased as the day warmed.

When Clait examined and measured the birds he caught, he made remarks about their condition—age, health, and what percentage of their feathers had molted. Examining one bird, he said, "She was a late breeder last summer."

"How can you tell?" I asked.

"The length of her tenth primary feather is shorter than normal. Primary feathers do not molt until after a hen has hatched her brood. Last summer she molted so late that her tenth primary never matured and remained shorter throughout the winter. She probably renested or had a late brood last summer."

The amount of information Clait gleans from his measurements continues to astound me. I will forever remain his student.

A female ptarmigan crouches, looking just like a rock.

~ June ~
COURTSHIP RITUALS AND NESTING

Sunshine is delicious, rain is refreshing, wind braces us up, snow is exhilarating; there is really no such thing as bad weather, only different kinds of good weather.

—John Ruskin

White-tailed ptarmigan perform courtship rituals amid the first wildflower blooms in the alpine tundra. Elevations of their breeding areas throughout the Rocky Mountains vary: in south-central Alaska, where timberline is about 3,500 feet, summer territories range from 4,000 to 5,000 feet; while in Colorado, birds are found between 10,900 to 13,900 feet, with territories of ten to eighty acres depending upon habitat quality.

By June, both male and female ptarmigan are in their nuptial plumage. It is the one time of year when it is relatively easy to distinguish the sexes. Males have a barred chest of white, black, and brown feathers, a brown and black mottled back, and a white underside. The female is more camouflaged, with brown, tan, and black feathers all over her body. When she crouches close to the ground it is almost impossible to see her.

The nuptial coloring of a male shows he is not a rock.

In early June a few years ago, I attended a seminar on Ptarmigan Ecology offered by the Rocky Mountain Nature Association and taught by Ken Giesen, another student of Clait Braun. In an area along Trail Ridge Road, with meadows, willows, and lingering snowbanks, Ken played a recording of a male territorial call. After a few moments, a male flew in to investigate. The bird looked around to check the invader, but as soon as he realized the recording was not another bird he walked away. He probably had a mate to protect. On another occasion, a lone male stayed near us, cackling loudly and challenging our recorded call.

On still another territory, the male bird clearly protected his mate, calling to her and keeping her within sight while we photographed and observed them. While male ptarmigan do not incubate eggs or help raise chicks, they do defend their territory and detract attention from the female.

Researchers Ray Schmidt, Kathy Martin, and Clait Braun detail the white-tailed ptarmigan courtship sequence as follows:

- **Courtship bow**—A male approaches a female while slowly bowing his head in a rhythmic pecking motion.
- **Courtship strut**—A male faces a female with neck inflated and red-orange eye combs flared, making him look larger. He fans his tail and tilts towards the hen, wing tips dragging on the ground.
- **Courtship chase**—A male holds his head upright, with eye combs flared, wings down, and tail fanned, while slowly approaching a female. As the female moves away, the male runs in pursuit. During the chase, the male utters clucks, chatters, and challenge calls.

These courtship behaviors cement the pair bond and precede mating. The female solicits copulation by squatting, lowering wings and tail, bobbing sideways, and wagging her head. The male approaches with a stiff-legged walk, grasps the back of the female's head and mounts. After mating, the hen moves away from the male and vigorously fluffs her body feathers while the male performs a strutting display. Copulation occurs multiple times during the breeding period.

While defending his territory, a male sits upon an outcrop cackling a strident call punctuated by bouncing aerial displays. If a male trespasses upon another's territory, the territorial male chases it away with great drama. I witnessed such a territorial dispute along Trail Ridge Road when a male not only chased the offending bird off his territory but also harassed the trespasser with loud shrieks during a quarter-mile downhill flight. The territorial male pursued the interloper like a jet fighter pilot, forcing the invader to retreat. The rightful owner then flew back uphill, sat upon his lookout rock, and cackled loudly, reasserting his territorial claim.

A cock faithfully protects and defends his territory, spending 90 percent of his time accompanying and guarding the hen. While guarding his mate, a male positions himself between an intruder and the hen and assumes an alert posture with eye combs extended. Defensive behaviors include flight screams, ground challenges, threat clucks, chatters, chirps, or stutter calls. Once, hiking up Mount Saint Vrain west of Allenspark, Colorado, I witnessed a male ptarmigan perform a distraction display. The cock repeatedly flew five to ten feet into the air and squawked loudly, moving toward me and then slightly to one side.

A male exhibits a courtship strut.

His ruse to distract me away from his mate worked; I was unable to find the female or her nest. A male white-tailed ptarmigan fends off intruders and stays on his territory until the eggs hatch.

In late June 1991, I went into the field on Mount Evans with researcher Kathy Martin where I witnessed the effectiveness of a bird dog. Kathy's dog, a pointer, had been trained to "freeze" after locating birds, allowing her to observe and subsequently to capture ptarmigan using noose poles or nets. Not wanting to disturb the process of pair bonding, courtship, and mating, Kathy delayed capturing females until they had spent several days on a territory with a particular male and the pair bond appeared stable.

To identify specific birds in her study of nesting success, Kathy placed colored bands on the legs of birds in her research area, using the system developed by Clait Braun. In addition, she placed a radio transmitter, designed as a collar, on all females and some males to enable her to monitor their mating status, nesting, and development. She classified birds as yearlings (less than one year old) or adults by examining their primary wing feathers. In first-year birds, the outer two primary wing feathers have small tan or brown splotches in the feather vane, whereas in adults these feathers are completely white. Being able to distinguish first-year birds from older birds allowed researchers to assess the mating success of individuals of different ages. By marking, tracking, and eventually recapturing birds, Kathy estimated that she and her students located more than 95 percent of the birds within her study area.

Using her dog and radio-collared birds proved invaluable in finding nests and in observing activities of the birds. In previous studies, researchers reported the difficulty of finding the nests, which were concealed very cryptically. No nests were found simply by searching for them within a territory. Ray Schmidt learned he could locate nests by watching territories of known pairs in late evening when hens left the nest to feed. Keeping these females in sight, Ray followed them as they walked back to their nests.

Nests on the ground in sites snowfree by early June may be located in rocky areas, in open meadows, next to willow shrubs, or by stunted conifers at timberline. Usually a well-hidden nest, protected from weather by a rock or vegetation, has an open escape route. Kathy found that most females select nest sites on their mate's territory, but sometimes the nests are at the edge or even off the territory.

Females do not begin nest activities until they are completely in their speckled, brown, and buff nuptial plumage. The timing of breeding and nesting events varies from year to year depending upon the weather. Molting of white winter feathers to summer plumage, triggered mainly by day length, is also influenced by the amount of snow on the ground and by the light intensity. A greater abundance of snow along with higher amounts of reflected

Kathy Martin uses a radio receiver to locate ptarmigan.

light delays molting and nesting, while little snow and a reduced amount of reflected light enhances earlier development. Plants also bloom earlier than normal in years with little spring snowfall and early melting; ptarmigan synchronize with earlier mating, nesting, and egg laying.

In years with early snowmelt, pairing occurs as early as the beginning of April, and the start of egg laying takes place during the first or second week of June. However, heavy spring snows delay pair bond formation until the middle of May, with egg laying beginning during the third or fourth week of June. Clait Braun reports that timing of nesting varies with locality as well as with climatic conditions for a particular year. For example, birds living on Mount Evans consistently nest earlier and young hatch about a week ahead of birds living along Trail Ridge Road in Rocky Mountain National Park, even though the two areas are less than a hundred miles apart and most of the territories on Mount Evans are at a higher elevation. Perhaps Mount Evans, although the top of the peak exceeds 14,000 feet, has a slightly milder climate with less snowfall because it does not straddle the Continental Divide.

When building her nest, a hen scrapes the ground with her beak and feet and pulls vegetation toward her body, forming a rim, repeating this activity during each nest visit. A female lines her nest with dried vegetation and feathers plucked from her breast. She lays one creamy-tan egg, faintly speckled with reddish-brown splotches, every day or two for about a week. After laying an egg the hen collects bits of surrounding vegetation, completely covering the egg before she leaves the nest. Average clutch size is six to seven, but can vary from four to nine. If an egg rolls away from the nest, the female may retrieve it by pulling it back into the nest with her beak.

The brown radio transmitter and antenna is attached to the bird on a specially designed necklace.

She ensures that chicks hatch at the same time by delaying incubation until all eggs have been laid. Once incubation begins, she plucks feathers from a highly vascularized area on her belly called a "brood patch." Having a naked patch on her belly allows heat to flow efficiently from her body to the eggs. A ptarmigan hen will spend more than 90 percent of her time on the nest during the twenty-two- to twenty-four-day incubation period, remaining still for hours, looking like a rock in the landscape.

A male defends his territory.

While ptarmigan often place their nests next to a rock or under a shrub for concealment and protection from wind or wet weather, the hen is often pelted with rain, sleet, or hail as she crouches low over her eggs. The male stays on the territory, usually just upslope of the nest, but rarely approaches the nest once the eggs are laid and the hen starts to incubate. During the incubation period, males will frequently join females during feeding times, especially at dusk.

Of the 248 nests in her study, Kathy found predators such as weasels, coyotes, red foxes, and—rarely—ravens destroyed two-thirds of them. In raids of nests, predators killed hens in addition to eating eggs nearly 10 percent of the time. Nests concealed by willows or sedges on all sides and without an escape route were especially vulnerable. Most nest predation occurred between 9 P.M. and 5 A.M., indicating that predators were nocturnal.

Weasels are fond of ptarmigan eggs and if a weasel (or other predator) disturbs a nest, the hen abandons it. If she is still early in the cycle of nesting and laying eggs, or has just started to incubate the eggs, she may construct a nest at a different site within the territory and start over again.

Ptarmigan hens, diligent in their job of laying and incubating eggs, remain on the breeding territory as eggs hatch and chicks start to develop. Males, however, depart once the young hatch, leaving the job of rearing chicks to the females.

A female on territory in June.

A ptarmigan pair on Niwot Ridge in July.

~ July ~

FAMILY TIME

Nature is only traditions: the turning of the seasons, of day and night, of sun and storm.

—Gaston Rebuffat, *Starlight and Storm*

The most difficult time to find ptarmigan is between mid-June and mid-July. During this period, females remain invisible when they sit quietly over their eggs, and while males remain on their territory, they rarely display during the nesting period. When I revisit an area where I saw breeding behavior a week before, I rarely see birds during the critical stage of incubation. Soliciting help from my students, I challenge them to find a ptarmigan nest, stating there will be a prize for the person who locates one. I describe the birds' habitat—lush alpine meadows with rocks and/or willow shrubs—and point toward an area to search. On July 6, 2005, a group of teachers and kids nine to ten years of age eagerly accepted my challenge and quickly ran up a slope to a ridge at 12,000 feet. When it was time to turn back and no birds had been located, I said, "Before we leave the alpine, let's check over there. If I were a ptarmigan, I'd make my home near that small pond, surrounded by rocks and lush vegetation."

Two boys raced toward the pond and suddenly stopped when one saw a bird. "There's a quail," he whispered loudly.

A female ptarmigan incubates her clutch.

"Not a quail—is it a ptarmigan?" the other asked.

I confirmed the bird was a male ptarmigan and pointed out his barred plumage. Then, sitting a couple yards from him, I saw a female, tan and more inconspicuous. I took pictures of the pair. Even though we did not find the elusive nest, we agreed that seeing a ptarmigan pair was a treat, a special prize for each of us.

If we had found a hen incubating her clutch, she would have remained vigilant but motionless. Approached too closely she may have flushed, and, in an effort to distract an intruder, she would have hissed, clucked, and exposed white underfeathers on her wings along with repeatedly advancing and retreating. Following a disruption, hens quickly return to their nests.

Being vigilant and sitting on her eggs day after day for twenty-two to twenty-four days finally pays off. The white-tailed ptarmigan hen hears clicking noises coming from her eggs. She responds with soft vocalizations. Within a day the hen may notice an egg pip, that is, the first pecking or breaking through, which occurs twenty-four to forty-eight hours before hatching. Newly hatched ptarmigan chicks are born with their eyes open; they are precocial, well developed, and fully feathered. Newborn chicks, covered by fuzzy down, weigh slightly more than one-half ounce (seventeen to nineteen grams), or about as much as three nickels.

Six to twelve hours after all chicks hatch, the hen leads them from the nest, never to return. The brown and tan fluffy chicks blend into their environment, and unless the chicks move, they are often overlooked. One year on July 15, I found a chick, probably only a day or two old, among the rocks on Mount Audubon. It seemed an almost impossible task for such a tiny bird to climb up and down the large boulders. The chick peeped frantically. Was it calling for its mother and asking her for a way down the large rock? Or was it a distress call?

Kathy Martin holds a one-day-old ptarmigan chick.

Although chicks are able to walk immediately after hatching, they do not regulate their body temperature well and still need to be protected by their mother. Ptarmigan hens are good mothers—they watch over their youngsters and make cooing and clucking sounds to call the chicks to duck beneath their feathered bodies for warmth and safety. Chicks brood under their mother at night to keep warm, and during the day she protects them from rain and wind or keeps them cool in the hot midday sun. Chicks forage at one day of age, and the hen often shows chicks a particular food by giving a low attraction call while pecking at the food item.

A hen alerts her chicks to danger.

Young chicks hide next to a rock.

A "craaow" call by their mom alerts chicks to danger, and they will either crouch low into the vegetation and remain motionless for up to thirty minutes or will scatter and hide under rocks. Unless I have seen chicks prior to hiding, they are impossible to find. And even when I have seen them crouch and hide, I sometimes lose them in a rock-strewn meadow.

Life for a young ptarmigan chick is full of hazards. Some wander too far from their mother and die from exposure. Weasels, coyotes, foxes, or raptors catch others. The odds for survival seem unlikely—over one-half of all nests fail and one-third of all chicks die within the first two weeks. However, a female only needs to produce two chicks that survive to adulthood during her lifetime for populations to remain stable.

One day, I watched Kathy Martin listen to her radio receiver as she twisted an antenna, first in one direction and then in another, to pinpoint a hen with a radio collar. Kathy picked up a signal, enabling her to walk toward the marked bird and her four small chicks.

Chick—ten to twelve days old.

Scooping up and placing each chick in a cloth bag, Kathy proceeded to weigh, measure, and then tag each youngster on one wing. While she worked, she kept other chicks beneath her sweater to keep them warm. Kathy did not release any chicks until she had finished recording her observations, because she had learned if she released them one at a time the hen would often walk away with an incomplete brood. "Ptarmigan can't count," Kathy explained. "If a hen sees one or two chicks she assumes that is her entire brood and will leave the others behind."

Ptarmigan chicks grow rapidly, doubling their birth weight in nine or ten days. Juvenile plumage gradually replaces down feathers. Eight gray primary-wing feathers become apparent between one and seven days. Ptarmigan chicks are able to fly by seven to ten days, and after seventeen to twenty-one days white primary-wing feathers start replacing the original eight gray primaries. By early September, the juvenile gray flight feathers molt completely and are replaced by white ones.

Signs of maleness occur early: this twelve-day-old chick shows an orange eye comb.

Ptarmigan feathers indicate a raptor has been successful.

Chicks triple their birth weight in three weeks, and then the hen only broods her chicks at night and during severe weather. She will allow the chicks to roam a little farther away from her during feeding periods.

After the eggs hatch, male ptarmigan abandon their breeding territories and move to higher meadows. Males congregate in rocky areas near melting snowbanks where vegetation remains moist and lush. Feeding on the summer's bounty, they steadily regain weight lost during courtship and territorial defense. Hens that have lost their brood also join males on these higher slopes.

From late July through August, hens with chicks are easier to find than earlier in the summer. A mother often sits upon a rock to watch her brood feed in a lush meadow. She establishes a safe area with clucks and coos, allowing chicks to roam twenty to thirty feet away. Chicks answer with a single syllable call, a high-pitched "cheerp" or lower-pitched, two-syllable "cheer-ups." However, when chicks wander too far or when danger threatens, the hen gives a "rally call." Occasionally chicks initiate a distress call with rapid "cheerps," "brrs," and "whets" and their mother responds by giving the rally call in return.

Communicating danger keeps ptarmigan safer from predators. Even so, I sometimes found signs of a kill. A pile of neatly plucked ptarmigan feathers in an area along Trail Ridge Road indicated that a raptor had hunted successfully. If the predator had been a mammal, the feathers would have been broken or chewed.

Young white-tailed ptarmigan chicks eat different foods than adults, feasting on insects, spiders, and other invertebrates. Grasshoppers, beetles, ants, and flies provide protein necessary for rapid growth. After two to three days, chicks add tender young leaves and flower petals to their diet. They seem to favor buttercups, clovers, and bulblets of viviparous bistort. As vegetation in their diet increases, chicks pick up and eat tiny bits of sharp rock. These rocks, called grit, stay in the bird's gizzard and help grind vegetation.

As a chick's diet changes, its digestive system changes and grows in length. When a chick is first hatched, the small intestine is well developed, enabling young birds to digest and absorb nutrients from its invertebrate diet as well as tender leaves and flowers. The caeca, two blind pouches containing bacteria and originating between the small and large intestines, which aid in the digestion of cellulose found in plant cell walls, do not enlarge for several weeks. By the end of the summer, however, these organs lengthen to accommodate the increased consumption of more fibrous material.

Unlike chicks, adults mostly eat plants. Early in the growing season, adults eat some insects but the bulk of their diet consists of plants. Some favorites include the flowers and leaves of snow buttercup, pasque flowers, dwarf clovers, and moss campions, as well as candy tuft, draba, and other mustards. A few weeks later as the alpine avens begins to flower, ptarmigan switch to avens, chickweed, snowball saxifrage, alpine and Parry's clover, and American bistort. The leaves and seed heads of American bistort, bulblets of viviparous bistort, and flowers of sedges are consumed during late July and August. As plants complete their reproductive cycle, the diet of ptarmigan changes from leaves and flowers to seeds. To conserve energy, ptarmigan eat a great deal at one time, storing food in their crop, and then rest motionless in rocky areas while the food passes into the gizzard where grit helps to grind food into digestible pieces. Much of the food is digested and absorbed in the small intestine, but the more fibrous material passes into the caeca where bacteria and protozoa promote digestion.

As the summer progresses, adults begin another molt. This molt from nuptial plumage to a neutral gray or brown coloration occurs after males have completed breeding and left their territories. Their coarsely barred feathers fade and are replaced with reticulated gray/brown feathers, giving the birds an overall gray appearance. Replacement feathers are finely speckled cinnamon to clay color with dark grayish brown flecks and thin bars. Females molt after the eggs hatch. By late summer, it is often difficult to distinguish females from males.

It seems curious that white-tailed ptarmigan molt almost continuously from late April to early November—in spring changing from winter to nuptial plumage, then in late summer to a neutral brownish-gray stage, and in autumn back to a winter coat. Because

Flowers in the ptarmigan's summer diet.

A ptarmigan hen with her two week old chick.

staying in tune with colors of their environment is so crucial, ptarmigan expend enormous energy molting three times every year.

July is family time. Changes occur rapidly. Eggs hatch and chicks grow at a fast pace, hens protect their broods, and males feed in high meadows. The alpine tundra in full bloom provides abundant food for accelerated activity in a brief period of warmth.

~ August ~
A SUMMER SURVEY
ON MOUNT EVANS

The alpine is my sanity.

—Clait Braun

*I*n early August many years ago I found a nest with four buff-colored eggs with darker splotches above timberline near Caribou Lake in the Indian Peaks Wilderness Area. This seemed too late for any bird to be nesting in the alpine and I took a picture. A decade later, I discovered it was a ptarmigan nest—and finding it so late in the summer made me realize the nest was undoubtedly a second attempt by a hen to raise a family. A ptarmigan hen lays fewer eggs when she renests, but the odds of survival for this brood were very slim as so little time remained in the summer for the chicks to get large enough to survive the winter conditions ahead.

Survival during the first few weeks is tenuous, but chicks that make it through their first month mature rapidly during August, exploiting the alpine's bounty. Hens with chicks often remain within a restricted neighborhood, enabling us to observe and photograph the same families repeatedly throughout the summer. In one area we found one hen with eight chicks and another with four chicks during late July. By the middle of August, both of these families had four chicks. One early

A ptarmigan nest with speckled eggs found in early August.

The chicks seem surprised when the hen leaves.

morning, the larger (and presumably the older) hen sat upon a rock, brooding her young, who wiggled beneath her feathery coat. Suddenly she got up and moved into the meadow to forage, leaving her surprised chicks.

Another hen with four chicks occupied a particularly lush meadow with a small pool along Trail Ridge Road. Early one morning, their reflections in the still water caught my attention—the young birds seemed to enjoy exploring and poking along the water's edge, much like young children.

Ptarmigan chick at the edge of a tundra pond.

Chicks develop rapidly during August.

By the end of August, most chicks are close to the size of adults. Families gradually move uphill toward summering areas occupied by males and females whose nests failed. Hens with chicks may stay somewhat separated from the main flock, especially if the hen is vigilant toward her young. Reproductive success in ptarmigan varies from 8 to 71 percent depending upon the amount of predation and weather conditions in a particular summer. One study reported higher nesting success in Rocky Mountain National Park as compared to Mount Evans.

A young chick displays eight gray primary wing feathers.

A hen with her chick in late August.

In late August I look forward to helping Clait Braun conduct an end-of-summer survey on Mount Evans. Standing tall in his faded blue jeans and battered sun hat, a noose pole in hand, Clait plays tape-recorded calls, alternating between males' territorial calls and chicks' distress cries. He listens for a response and then walks on, repeating the call and listening. At this time of year birds do not always react to calls. Sometimes we locate birds simply by hiking through their habitats and looking for movement.

Because ptarmigan flock together during late August and early September, they are easy to detect, and it is not uncommon to see twenty-five or thirty birds in a group. They move higher on the mountain than in previous months, and some are found as high as within 300 feet of the 14,000-foot-high summit of Mount Evans.

On August 23, 2005, I helped Clait on the fourth day of his weeklong survey; he had already found sixty to seventy birds. The first birds we found that morning were a yearling hen that weighed 350 grams (12 ounces) and two chicks, weighing 260 and 268 grams

Clait snares a male chick during his survey.

(9 to 9.5 ounces). Measuring the length and color of the primary wing feathers on the chicks, Clait was able to determine their ages. From previous studies he determined that chicks first grow eight gray primary feathers and later add primary nine and ten, which grow in white. New feathers grow at a rate of 6.3 millimeters per day. Measuring the size and coloration of the primary feathers on the chick, Clait determined the chicks had hatched between July 5 and 10 and were six to seven weeks old. One of the chicks was probably a male as he already had a larger orange eye comb.

Clait talked quietly as he measured the birds and took notes on the condition of each bird's beak and toenails. The sheath over the beak is usually shed during August or September, revealing a new beak tip. Having a sharper beak is an obvious preparation for winter, making it possible for a bird to nip off hard willow buds and stems. Toenails dulled by walking over rocks all summer are also shed, allowing new, sharper ones to grow in preparation for digging in hard snowdrifts during winter.

In a rocky area nearer the summit of Mount Evans, we found a flock with at least twelve to fifteen birds that Clait had previously banded, along with four males and two females without bands. First, using binoculars, we recorded the color sequence of the leg bands, as this information would enable Clait to determine the bird's age and history. The oldest banded bird, a nine-year-old male, had originally been captured as a yearling in 1997. Clait then captured the birds with no bands—weighing, measuring, and banding each one before releasing it. Collecting this data over many years enables Clait to track trends in ptarmigan populations.

Sometimes Clait handed a bird to me to look at and admire before releasing it. I saw the beauty of the feathers, felt the softness, the warmth of the body; I smelled the bird's odor, and stared into its eye before setting it upon the ground. Birds tolerated our gentle handling and would usually just walk away from us when released. Half of the birds we saw were under four years of age, but some birds do reach an old age—the longevity record goes to a twelve-year-old male.

The bird is weighed.

The next day we found one hen with three chicks and a yearling male, a suitor in waiting, Clait explained. "Ptarmigan are social birds, and yearling males often hang out with a female and her chicks in late summer. This male is probably not the father of her brood, but he is advertising to the hen that he is available for next year."

Clait explained that successful hens go back to their same territory, and if their previous mates are still living they will breed again. "But," he added, "if the male dies and

Clait measures and takes note of the color and development
of primary wing feathers to determine the chick's age.

does not return, this yearling will have a chance at the unoccupied territory, and may father her next brood."

Often while watching ptarmigan, I see them preen. Since keeping their feathers in good alignment and picking out dirt and parasites is such an important activity, birds preen many times every day. In addition, ptarmigan take dust baths in summer, fluttering their wings in a dirt pile. One afternoon, I watched dust fly over the head and between the feathers of a female as she flapped her wings over and over again. Her bath cleaned excess oils and dirt from the feathers. Then she shook and vigorously fluffed up her feathers and used her beak to poke all over, realigning and combing her feathered coat. When birds molt, the amount of time spent on preening increases. They scratch themselves with long toenails and pull out old feathers with their beaks.

Some birds fly when they are released.

A ptarmigan dust bathing.

A ptarmigan preens, keeping its feathers in top condition.

Pika

Marmot

Toward the end of August, autumn creeps into the alpine: alpine gentians bloom, dryas seeds catch the morning sun, and alpine avens leaves tint the landscape scarlet. The summer wanes. Pika, small rock rabbits of the tundra, frantically increase gathering vegetation, placing it in hay piles to be used as winter fodder. Marmots, too, prepare for the change in season, eating continuously and storing fat beneath their skin to sustain them during their winter hibernation.

In 2005 on the last day of his survey, Clait Braun announced that he had completed a forty-year study on Mount Evans and it was time to step down. Musing about his work, he said, "There are now almost twice as many birds on Mount Evans as there were in 1966. Hunting was banned within a half-mile of the road in the 1990s, allowing the population to soar. This has been a good year. Back in 1904, Evan Lewis wrote about ptarmigan nesting on Mount Evans, and I wrote about them in 2004; I hope these birds will still be the focus of someone's study in 2104, a hundred years from now."

Sitting upon a rock in September, a ptarmigan basks in the last days of clear skies and warm temperatures.

SHORTER DAYS SIGNAL A CHANGE OF SEASON

Ptarmigan are evolutionary wonders, masters of disguise who would rather switch than fight. As winter comes on with its shorter days, glandular reactions signal the replacement of mottled summer-brown feathers with snow-white plumage.

—Ken Marsh, *"Searching for Snow Grouse"*

Summer comes to an end, nights become longer and cooler, frost coats the vegetation, and seeds ripen. Arctic gentians continue to bloom through the first snows. The weather swings between snowstorms and sunny, warm days; the alpine glows scarlet, tan, and yellow. Some of the most enjoyable "Indian Summer" days lie ahead.

Before the alpine takes on winter's cloak, some animals migrate, others hibernate, and a few remain active and develop a resistance to the bitter cold. Migration seems like an easy way to avoid harsh weather, but migration has its own demands. It is costly in terms of energy expended. If migrating birds, for example, fail to accumulate sufficiently large fat reserves, they will not have enough energy to complete their journey. However, migration allows those species strong and mobile

A hen feasts on bistort seeds.

enough a way of utilizing the high mountain environment during favorable periods and lowland or other habitats during more stressful times.

Most birds cannot cope with the lower temperatures and diminished food of an alpine winter and must migrate. Shorter days spur movement in American pipits, horned larks, rosy finches, and white-crowned sparrows. White-crowned sparrows and horned larks retreat to lower elevations of the foothills and plains, while rosy finches descend only a couple of

A ptarmigan chick peeks out through autumn-colored vegetation.

thousand feet to subalpine or montane habitats. American pipits travel the farthest, to the southern United States or Mexico.

As some birds and mammals move into foothill canyons, others such as bluebirds, flickers, and western meadowlarks migrate up in fall, feeding on abundant insects. They stay in the alpine only a few weeks, moving down when temperatures fall. Some raptors such as northern harriers and prairie falcons also migrate to the alpine in September, to hunt rodents and even ptarmigan at the peak of their population.

One alpine bird remains a resident year-round—our indefatigable white-tailed ptarmigan. During September, hens with nearly adult-sized chicks inhabit rocky alpine areas near pockets of moisture below late-lying snowfields. They eat dryas leaves, mat plants, viviparous bistort, alpine sorrel, sedges, seeds of American bistort, and arctic gentians. Often broods begin to disperse, wandering off to congregate with other broods. Some hens will actually adopt chicks from other broods. One hen that had three chicks in

A chick hides in the rocks.

A chick drinks water in a small rock pool.

August guarded a brood of eight in September made up of different-sized chicks. "Some anxious mothers remain vigilant and add chicks to their family while other hens allow their brood to wander away," Clait Braun explains.

I relish the change of season; I love to hike on clear, crisp autumn days with deep blue skies. The colorful foliage of the alpine rivals the eastern deciduous forests, and cooler temperatures are invigorating. Days with low humidity make colors more brilliant. It was on such a day that I followed a family of ptarmigan along Trail Ridge Road. It almost seemed as if the birds and I played a game of hide-and-seek as they wandered through the rock-studded meadows, eating sedge and bistort seeds. Green and tan sedges, maroon leaves of alpine avens, and white, puffy seed heads of mountain dryas provided the backdrop canvas. The birds wandered, pecking at the vegetation while I took photographs. What a glorious day!

Another September day, I searched for the ptarmigan I had been following all summer on Mount Audubon in the Indian Peaks Wilderness. There were no birds at 12,000 feet where they had nested and raised their young. I could not find them in the moist meadows, near the willows, or in rock-studded dry meadows. Again the elusive birds had evaded me. I continued to the peak's summit.

On my way down the mountain, just a few hundred feet above treelimit, I heard a soft cooing. There, almost in front of me, were five ptarmigan feeding on bistort and arctic gentians. They had not started their autumn molt yet, probably because there had been little snow. Their plumage looked like it had in August and they blended in with rocks in the alpine meadow, but the birds had started to move down the mountainside.

In September large flocks of ptarmigan appear more nervous and become disturbed easily, flying up to a hundred yards before settling down. This agitated behavior, also seen in other grouse species during this time of year, indicates the birds are preparing to migrate to more protected areas in anticipation of winter.

Along Trail Ridge Road, I found within a group of thirty birds in a rocky area a banded bird that looked like it was a large male. I wondered about its age and took its picture, which

In September, birds of both sexes flock together.

Banded male near Trail Ridge Road.

I e-mailed to Clait Braun that evening. The next day I had my answer: the bird was eight years old and had been banded in the same area in 1998. It was fun to feel that I had contributed some data about ptarmigan living in Rocky Mountain National Park.

Caught in the first snowstorm of the season on another autumn outing, I encountered high winds and snow that quickly turned the alpine white. Every plant stem and blade of grass had a coating of rime, and wind cut through my fleece jacket. Approaching Arapahoe Ridge, I put on a wind parka with a hood to prevent icy shards from abrading my face. The flat light made it difficult to see features of the landscape.

I came out of the fog and saw two speckled birds walking downhill. Their fluffed-up feathers made them look like round balls. Unlike usual sightings when the birds blend into their surroundings, these ptarmigan contrasted with the white scene. I stopped and watched and counted five more birds emerging from the mist. The speckled birds had barely started their autumn molt—only feathers on their lower belly were white, the rest appeared mottled. With the first severe snow, the ptarmigan moved downhill; a few days later if the weather moderated, they would go back up, returning to summering areas. During these

After the first snow's, we find tracks of ptarmigan.

first snowstorms, ptarmigan are especially vulnerable to predation because they do not blend with their surroundings.

Shorter days trigger the release of hormones that provide the signal for ptarmigan to begin molting. White feathers appear first along their flank, and the birds grow an extra undercoat of down as well as new contour feathers. The amount of snow on the ground influences the rate of molting, and if a particular autumn has little snow, ptarmigan delay molting for several weeks. Gradually,

Autumn molting begins from the bottom of the bird and moves upward.

The alpine in autumn coloration.

however, dark feathers on their back and neck are replaced with white ones. In autumn, the molt in ptarmigan progresses from bottom to top in contrast with their head to bottom spring molt.

Frequently juveniles acquire white feathers earlier than the adults. Young ptarmigan, even though they are nearly adult-sized, are still readily distinguished from adults as they have shorter tail feathers, and their newly formed white feathers are interspersed with finely barred tan feathers. Even through their first winter, juveniles can be recognized because their outer two white primary wing feathers display darker vanes.

The number of birds I saw along Trail Ridge Road during any one day in September varied from a flock of thirty birds to no birds following a snowstorm. I believed the birds had left the high alpine, but two weeks later I saw a hen with three juveniles that apparently had walked back uphill during a period of warmer weather. To one who is constantly on the move up and down, autumn marks a season of change and transition—a burst of glory that gradually fades as snow and cold moves into the land.

By early October, a chick (right) is as large as its mother (left).

SELECTING A
WINTER HOME

I feel lucky by a chance encounter—
Elusive in their habits and camouflage,
In winter hiding in white drifts,
In summer looking like rocks in an alpine meadow.
But my favorite time is in autumn
When white feathers start to replace speckled ones.
At edges of snow patches,
Blending into dried grasses and splotches of white,
White-tailed ptarmigan, masters of disguise,
Give me a glimpse into their unique place
As tundra dwellers.

—Joyce Gellhorn

When the alpine tundra becomes dappled by snow, tracks on newly formed drifts sometimes help me locate ptarmigan. Other times, tracks tell me where birds have been even though I do not see them. Additionally, I look for signs I usually find during winter—tracks, scat, and depressions where birds have dug into the snow and roosted for the night.

Along Trail Ridge Road in the beginning of October, I scan areas with gentle swales where willows grow. Here, early snows start to form small drifts. I find a line of faint scratches on hard snow that indent deeper where the drift becomes softer. Finally, I notice the telltale tracks: three toes pointing forward and one toe pointing back. I do not see any birds, but I keep walking, stopping at intervals to look around. Ten minutes later, I see more tracks going in different directions. Some are headed for taller vegetation, and I hunt closer to shrubs and small tree islands. A bird hunkers by the edge of a snowdrift; then I see another and another. I follow them as they walk uphill, and then I sit down as the birds settle and peck at vegetation in the meadow. A female and three almost fully grown chicks blend in with

As a bird begins to molt to winter-white plumage, it stands out in the snow.

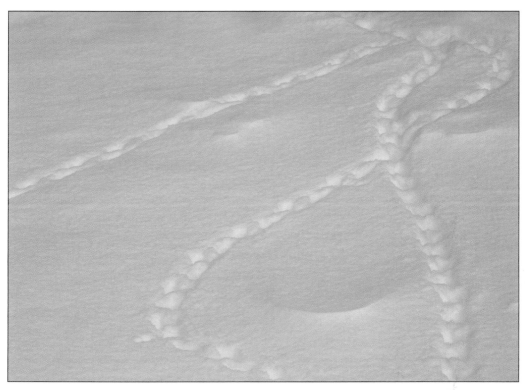

Tracks in soft snow.

the snow and dried grasses. The birds seem to know they are more visible on snow, for they dart across snow patches quickly; but they slow to a walk once they reach rocks or dried vegetation.

The pace of the afternoon slows as the birds and I sit and study one another. The birds eat for a time, and then sit with their feathers puffed up. I, too, sit quietly, and the birds approach me until they are no more than an arm's-length away. Slowly I reach out and barely touch their feathered backs and look into their eyes. It's a magical moment. Everything is quiet, peaceful—just the ptarmigan and me in the beauty of the alpine tundra.

On another October outing I discover five ptarmigan just above treelimit near Blue Lake in the Indian Peaks Wilderness. In the middle of their molt from summer to winter plumage, some seek edges of the snow where they blend in with their surroundings while others hunch almost invisibly next to willow shrubs. The combination of pure white feathers with delicately barred tan and mottled ones captivates me.

A bird on a rock shows off its feathered legs and feet.

These birds, like the ones on Trail Ridge, appear docile and allow me to approach closely. Yet they are aware, their eyes following me as I shift position. As the snow changes from soft and fluffy to icy and wind-packed, tracks of the ptarmigan look different. When the new snow is not too deep, lines of tracks indent the surface, with toes on each footprint clearly visible. Drag marks from toenails sometimes show between the footprints. Because a snowdrift may consist of snow of different densities, tracks may sometimes be visible and then suddenly disappear. When tracks age, they take on a different look as the wind, sun, and changes in temperature affect the snow surface.

Throughout the month, more and more white feathers appear in a ptarmigan's feathery robe. Feathers also grow upon the feet, increasing their surface area four to five times over nonfeathered feet. This enables birds to walk upon quite soft snow without sinking. Tracks made by "snowshoed" feet look larger than one might expect for a bird slightly larger than a pigeon.

In preparation for the oncoming winter, a ptarmigan's toenails increase in length, providing sharper ends that give them traction when the snow surface becomes hard and icy. Long toenails enable birds to dig into the snowpack to form burrows where they roost.

A ptarmigan's feathered feet act like snowshoes.

Male elk spar to establish dominance.

As autumn gives way to winter, willow buds and stems again become the mainstay of the ptarmigan's diet. To aid in the digestion of this woody material, birds ingest small, sharp grit particles at windblown, snow-free sites. These particles pass into the gizzard where they abrade tough food into digestible pieces. In addition, the bird's crop, large intestine, and caeca enlarge during this season to provide greater efficiency in food collection and nutrient absorption. The high fibrous content of winter browse reduces its digestibility, thus requiring additional food intake. An enlarged crop enables a bird to rapidly gather and store food, usually during short morning and evening foraging bouts. In the enlarged caeca, tough plant cellulose is digested during periods of seeming inactivity, times when birds roost in snowy burrows.

While seeking ptarmigan, I often have opportunities to see the activity of other animals. In preparation for winter, bull elk bugle and gather herds of females for mating. Males display their fine antlers and spar with each other to establish dominance. I am reminded that there are other reasons for hiking in the alpine than to look for elusive birds.

As winter approaches, ptarmigan flocks segregate into all-male bands, groups of females, and juvenile flocks of both sexes. Male bands with fewer than fifteen individuals remain above 11,500 feet. Females travel to willow basins at or below timberline, forming flocks of twenty to eighty birds intermingling with groups of immature birds.

Winter, lasting for six months from late October to late April, marks a time when ptarmigan hide in the snow near willow stands. Birds rarely venture away from wintering sites; it is a time for birds to feed, rest, and hunker down, staying out of the worst weather tucked in a snow shelter, winter's insulating blanket.

As winter approaches, birds seek out habitat with willows.

A sleeping bird shows its feathered eyelids.

~November~
COLDER TEMPERATURES

**And now there came both mist and snow,
And it grew wondrous cold.**

—Samuel Taylor Coleridge,
"The Rime of the Ancient Mariner"

November typically brings heavier snow, wind, and colder temperatures. To adjust to this weather, people wear long johns under ski pants, warm parkas, and hats and gloves, and they drink hot toddies following an outing. White-tailed ptarmigan move away from exposed, wind-scoured ridgetops and slopes to snowier environs. Soft snow is critical to winter survival, particularly the soft snow blown by wind to the lee of rocks and clumps of vegetation.

More than 70 percent of ptarmigan observed during November and throughout the winter are in and around willows because the birds use the shrubs for both food and shelter. On days with especially strong winds, however, birds abandon these habitats because snow becomes too hard to dig good roosts. As ptarmigan researcher Terry May found, "In the absence of suitable snow for roosting in major feeding areas, ptarmigan wintering at or above tree line have been observed to fly downhill for at least half a mile to spend the night in the softer snow."

Different types of feathers cloak a ptarmigan's body: contour (left), down (upper right), semiplume with afterfeather (lower right).

A bird in early November still has a few feathers on its wing that have not molted.

Designed for existence in a hostile climate, the ptarmigan's white plumage retains body heat. Feathers keep birds warm both by their thickness and by trapping air. An extra coat of down in their winter plumage provides an efficient insulator. People, in spite of sophisticated technology, still have not been able to design a better material against cold.

Birds have many different types of feathers: contour feathers cover the bird's body. These feathers have a central axis or rachis and vanes with interlocking barbules that "zip" together to keep the feather firm. Underneath contour feathers are short, fluffy down feathers that provide insulation. Down feathers, lacking hooked barbules, promote loft because the vanes do not zip together. Semiplumes fall between contour feathers and down feathers, combining a large central rachis with downy vanes at the bottom and a stiffer tip. Longer than down feathers, semiplumes fill in or smooth out the various contours of a bird's body while insulating it.

A bird displays its rotund shape, a result of piloerection of its feathers.

Afterfeathers, another type of feather, are more numerous in ptarmigan than in other birds. Afterfeathers grow out from the main feather axis of contour or semiplume feathers, increasing both the quantity of feathers and their insulative quality. The afterfeathers of ptarmigan in winter, three-fourths as long as the feathers from which they originate, provide an extra layer of highly branched downy filaments with noninterlocking barbs that contain air pockets. The numerous afterfeathers add additional loft and contribute to the thickness of a ptarmigan's plumage, making them appear rotund.

Because contour feathers are white in winter, their central axis lacks pigment. This leaves a dead air space in the rachis, which further insulates the white birds. Even the ptarmigan's nostrils and eyelids are feathered. Feathered nostrils, like hairs in our nasal passages, help warm the air before it enters the lungs. Feathers on the eyelids cover and insulate a small portion of skin covering the eyes that otherwise might be vulnerable to cold air.

Finally, muscles connected to feather tracts enable birds to fluff themselves up to trap more air when it is cold, a mechanism called "piloerection." Piloerection enables birds to maintain a high body temperature even when outside temperatures become frigid. With their feathered cloak, ptarmigan have evolved a lightweight and maneuverable winter robe, one that cannot be exceeded.

As I search for ptarmigan in November among snowdrifted willow bogs in the Indian Peaks Wilderness Area, I sink deeply in the new snow even with snowshoes. I follow my usual routine: I walk, stop, and look—again and again. The day is cold but not too windy. I am in the birds' winter habitat, but where are the birds? Finally, I see a telltale sign—tracks lead from a depression in the snow filled with droppings. More tracks sink only a couple of inches compared to my snowshoe tracks of a couple feet. Oh, to be a light bird with feathered feet! A surface area of their feathered feet, increased four times over unfeathered feet, enables ptarmigan to sink less than half as far into the snow. Not only does this allow birds to stay on top of the snow, it also reduces the energy required for walking.

Finding tracks does not always mean I find birds, but today I am lucky. Birds feed among the willows—white against white with black beaks and black eyes. They look at me but seem unperturbed by my presence. Some still have a few black feathers around their eyes, the last feature to molt to the winter plumage.

A few black feathers around the eyes are the last to molt.

The birds feed, roost, and relax among the willows. One bird shakes around in a newly constructed roost. It is taking a snow bath. Snow flies above its head as the bird forces snow between its feathers to clean them. The bird shakes itself energetically. More snow flies. All of a sudden, another bird comes over and nudges the bird out of its hollow. The second bird proceeds to take a snow bath in the first one's spot. Following the snow bath, both ptarmigan preen their feathers with their beaks and feet, realigning all their feathers and zipping the barbules back together.

The gregariousness of ptarmigan seems most evident from late October until late April when birds gather in large numbers on wintering sites. Some sites used by ptarmigan early in the winter are devoid of birds later in the season when increasing snow depths cover the willow shrubs. The birds move to areas of taller willows where the tips remain snowfree. As spring approaches and the snow settles, exposing unused buds, birds often reoccupy areas previously abandoned.

One flock in the Indian Peaks Wilderness Area probably has twelve to twenty individuals; frequently I find groups of four to six at one time. One year I followed a group of four

Ptarmigan snow bathing.

Ptarmigan preening.

throughout the entire season. I identified them because one had a distinctly hooked beak. Although "Hook" was not as photogenic as her companions, she served as an identifying marker to the flock. The deformity did not prevent her from eating, and she seemed vigorous. The group ranged through an area about a half-mile long. While I did not find the group on every outing, when I did they allowed me to photograph their activities and I looked upon them as friends.

"Hook."

~December~
A TIME TO
CONSERVE ENERGY

Two white-tailed ptarmigan in ermine robes
Stand facing each other
As I photograph their regal postures.
With soft clucks they
Keep track of each other.
And to me they say,
"You are no threat,
You cannot see us,
We blend into the snow,
We are invisible."

—Joyce Gellhorn

hite-tailed ptarmigan seem oblivious to the harshness of winter as long as they have snow in which to make snug hollows. Long before Eskimos built igloos, ptarmigan mastered the art of snow-cave construction. Birds within roosts in the snowpack are protected from wind and cold from sundown to sunup, a period of fourteen hours. Birds also dig into the snow during the day in severe weather to protect themselves from windchill. In prolonged storms, ptarmigan also spend most of their day beneath the snow surface without moving. Periodically, they rouse themselves and make short

A ptarmigan stretches.

runs, flapping their wings repeatedly. After stretching, they will feed before selecting another resting spot.

Birds unable to find suitable snow in which to burrow during long winter nights cannot maintain their high body temperature and will die from exposure. Thus, winters with lower-than-average snowfall can be more devastating to ptarmigan populations than a snowy year.

In light, fluffy snow, ptarmigan shake their body and sink to make a roost; in harder drifts they dig with their beak and sharp toenails. An icy snow surface inhibits burrowing, leading to speculations that ptarmigan will dive into hard drifts to break through the crust with their sturdy breast. Clait Braun feels that is a myth. "Instead," Clait says, "they fly or walk to a suitable area, then dig into the snow with scratching movements of their feet while pushing themselves into the depression with lateral, shaking movements of the body." Sometimes flocks have to move downhill to krummholz trees that catch softer windblown snow for their nightly roosts. On the lee side of one krummholz, I found fourteen forms, depressions where ptarmigan had spent the night. I called these "snow condominiums."

While some roosts appear as small scrapes, others go down a foot or more and tunnel several feet laterally. I have seen ptarmigan stick their head up through the snow from a roost that is completely covered over. I have skied so close to a buried bird that it bursts in flight through the surface. Imagine my fright by an explosion of feathers between my skis! Usually ptarmigan only fly fifteen to twenty yards and then settle down again. Other birds in the flock, not disturbed by the pressure of my skis, would peck a hole in the overlying snow and climb out of their roost to see what was going on.

During a particularly cold and snowy December I skied in the Indian Peaks Wilderness to check my ptarmigan. I saw nothing. Day after day I was stymied. The windblown snow erased their tracks, the cold confined them to snow burrows, and even on a day less windy than the rest, I did not find any birds. I skied among the willows, looked under krummholz trees, and tried to think like a ptarmigan. Learning more and more about the birds and their habits does not always mean I find them. Perhaps their elusiveness is what I find attractive. I always feel a sense of adventure in looking for them and even when they remain hidden, I have a memorable outing.

"Snow condominiums" on the lee side of krummholz trees.

A ptarmigan's head barely peeks above the snow surface.

Clear, calm, warm winter days sometimes inhibit ptarmigan activity as much as excessive wind and snow. During balmy periods, birds will feed for a couple of hours early in the morning, and then roost for most of the day, becoming active again at dusk. Ptarmigan easily fulfill their energy requirements in the two-hour morning and evening foraging sessions. On overcast days, however, birds feed most of the time, seemingly to stock up for harsher conditions ahead. Fat reserves of 3 to 5 percent allow birds to subsist for two days with a full crop.

Roosting birds, unlike hibernating mammals, remain alert with a high metabolic rate. If the temperature in the snow burrow remains 5° F or so warmer than the surrounding snow and perhaps 25° F warmer than the air above the snowpack, a bird saves as much as 45 percent in heat loss. This allows ptarmigan to maintain a constant body temperature with minimal expenditures of energy.

Winter-white ptarmigan need to adapt to changing snow conditions that occur throughout the season. Freshly fallen snow consists largely of air and only a small bit of solid material, the ice crystals. New snow at high elevations of the Rocky Mountains has a density around 7 percent with a snow-to-water ratio of fourteen to one, that is, fourteen inches of snow equals one inch of water. As snow ages it compacts, and wind-beaten snow with icy layers becomes even denser. Even so, the blanket of snow covering the ground contains life-sustaining air pockets within its crystal lattice that ptarmigan depend on in their snowy roosts. The many-layered snowpack changes continually in response to seasonal events: storms bring more snow, alternations in temperature, and wind.

On the snow's surface I look for signs of other animals as well. Sometimes I see tracks of predators such as foxes, coyotes, and weasels. In winter, ptarmigan seem more wary of

Four sleepers.

these carnivores than in other seasons and flocks often flush when they sight predators, flying as far as a mile away.

On a recent December survey on Guanella Pass, Rick Hoffman asked me to be the leader in searching for ptarmigan in Section 2. I organized our group, telling new members what to look for and spacing people in a line twenty yards apart as we snowshoed through the area. The weather had been cold and windy and I predicted that we would see more birds during our second sweep where softer snow offered the birds more protection. "Also look carefully around the krummholz tree islands as birds often snow roost in these areas," I said. "You may call to one another when you see birds because they are generally not disturbed by us as long as we stay at least ten feet away."

Tony, a lanky volunteer and avid birder who had never seen ptarmigan, was about forty feet upslope from me when he saw the first group of four birds. "Birds!" he shouted. The birds, often described as phlegmatic and not easily disturbed, promptly spooked and flew. They landed about twenty yards away so all eight members of the survey team could

Surveyors start out on a windy day on Guanella Pass.

Ghost bird.

gather around to observe them. But the skittish birds certainly did not behave in the manner I had predicted.

About an hour later, Susan, a volunteer living in Georgetown, spotted a group of seven birds. Not knowing her location, someone asked Susan over the walkie-talkie to wave so he could see where the birds were. Susan waved vigorously with hands over her head, startling the feeding ptarmigan into flight before I was able to photograph them. Birds in both sightings acted differently and were not in areas I had expected, letting me know I still have much to learn.

Following white-tailed ptarmigan has inspired adventures to many of my favorite places. It has allowed me to observe nature closely through all months of the year and to ponder the trials and tribulations of another species. With gratitude I thank these remarkable ghosts for all they have taught me about adapting to their high country home in the Rocky Mountains.

EPILOGUE:
WHAT'S AHEAD FOR THE PTARMIGAN?

We are a part of the Creation—the living world—in body and spirit. We belong on this planet as a biological heritage, and we have a sacred personal duty to keep it intact and healthy.

—E. O. Wilson

Wilderness itself is the basis of all our civilization. I wonder if we have enough reverence for life to concede to wilderness the right to live?

—Margaret "Mardy" Murie

According to historical accounts of white-tailed ptarmigan, these birds were common in alpine areas of Colorado when the first white men arrived. Dr. W. Anderson, a naturalist on Captain R. B. Macy's expedition from Fort Bridger to Santa Fe, New Mexico, collected birds on January 2, 1858, near Cochetopa Pass (elevation 12,000 feet) in western Saguache County, sending specimens to the Smithsonian Institution. This collection of white-tailed ptarmigan extended the known range for the species over 1,000 miles southward.

During the period from the 1870s to 1890, numerous sightings of ptarmigan in all of Colorado's high-altitude mountain ranges reported their seasonal plumage changes. Some collections were extensive, and one included over 1,000 birds.

Extensive collections may have diminished local ptarmigan populations. Later, grazing by domestic livestock compromised the health of alpine ecosystems, and sheep grazing on ptarmigan breeding grounds further reduced and degraded habitat for the birds. Ptarmigan populations declined drastically. These birds, often noted for their docile nature, were killed for sport by people throwing stones or sticks at them.

While ptarmigan are still listed as game birds, hunting is now prohibited within a half-mile of the road on Mount Evans, reversing the precipitous decline of ptarmigan in that area in the 1980s and 1990s. The population now appears to be stable.

Over many years of studying white-tailed ptarmigan, I have become very protective of the birds. Imagine my disappointment at not finding any signs of "my birds" during the winter of 2003 after years of observing winter flocks near a lake in the Indian Peaks Wilderness Area. Instead of finding ptarmigan, I saw telltale signs of moose—moose droppings and willows heavily browsed and trampled by large feet. In the late 1970s, the Division of Wildlife transplanted moose, not native to Colorado, into Jackson County. Finding suitable habitat, moose populations grew and they expanded their range to the Front Range. In many areas moose out-compete other wildlife—providing another example in which introducing nonnative species has had a negative impact upon native ecosystems.

Throughout that winter I kept going back again and again to check on the status of the birds, hoping that they would return, and being disappointed at not finding them. Clearly the moose, feeding upon the same resource as ptarmigan, had displaced the birds.

As winter approached the following year, I was eager to find out who would inhabit the ptarmigan's favored willow habitat. Near the end of October there was just enough snow to ski, and although the day was windy and I did not see any birds, I saw forms, ptarmigan overnight roosts, filled with their droppings. My birds were back—I was overjoyed.

A few weeks later on a bird survey of Rainbow Lakes Valley, I saw signs of moose. The moose were now occupying a different locale than in 2003, which allowed the ptarmigan to return to their previous wintering habitat.

A similar situation has occurred in Rocky Mountain National Park. Elk, although native, were reintroduced to the Estes Park area after they had been hunted nearly to extinction in the early 1900s. By then, predators of elk that served to regulate their numbers had also been eliminated. As elk populations soared, they required greater areas to forage. Many bull elk and later mixed herds began to stay in alpine areas during winter—areas from which they had seasonally migrated. The elk's diet during winter included more shrubs, damaging the willows that ptarmigan depend upon in winter. As elk populations increased, the delicate balance of alpine ecosystems became disrupted and ptarmigan populations declined.

Over the past 150 years, ptarmigan have been impacted by other human activities: mining caused heavy metals to leach into wetlands, suitable ptarmigan habitat has diminished due to more hiking trails and roads into alpine areas, and global warming has changed climates.

Willows damaged by the browsing of elk in alpine areas along Trail Ridge Road impact wintering areas for ptarmigan.

One metal whose effects have been studied is cadmium, a trace metal in ore-bearing rock. As cadmium-rich water leached from mine slag piles into wetlands, it was taken up and concentrated in willows. Ptarmigan that ate willow buds contaminated by cadmium laid fewer eggs, their eggshells were more fragile, and their young had higher mortality rates. Luckily, in some contaminated areas, ptarmigan populations have begun to rebound as mine sites have been reclaimed.

Recreation is the fastest-growing cause of disturbance to alpine landscapes and wildlife. Increased direct confrontation between ptarmigan and people can negatively affect the birds. One winter day at a lake in the Indian Peaks Wilderness Area I skied to the east end and stood, admiring clouds swirling around the mountain peaks and snow patterns on the ice. Looking toward the south side of the lake, I saw a dog with a red pack chasing back and forth in the willows barking and barking. Suddenly, three white birds rose into the air.

DISTRIBUTION OF SEASONAL RANGES OF WHITE-TAILED PTARMIGAN IN RELATION TO ELEVATION, TOPOGRAPHY, AND MAJOR VEGETATIONAL TYPES

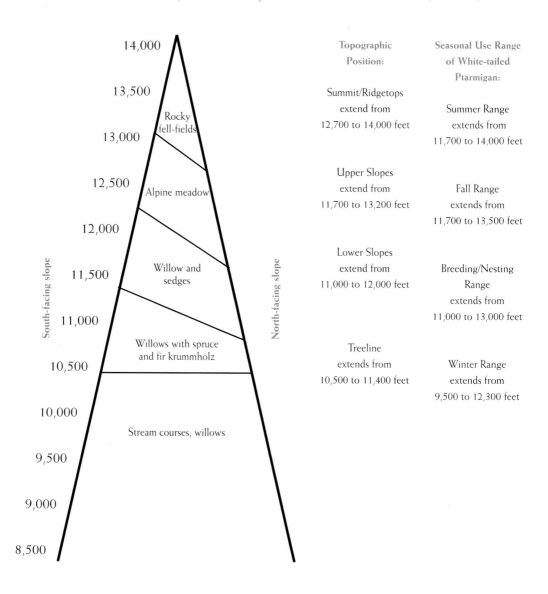

14,000

13,500

13,000 — Rocky fell-fields

12,500 — Alpine meadow

12,000

11,500 — Willow and sedges

11,000

10,500 — Willows with spruce and fir krummholz

10,000

9,500 — Stream courses, willows

9,000

8,500

South-facing slope

North-facing slope

Topographic Position:

Summit/Ridgetops extend from 12,700 to 14,000 feet

Upper Slopes extend from 11,700 to 13,200 feet

Lower Slopes extend from 11,000 to 12,000 feet

Treeline extends from 10,500 to 11,400 feet

Seasonal Use Range of White-tailed Ptarmigan:

Summer Range extends from 11,700 to 14,000 feet

Fall Range extends from 11,700 to 13,500 feet

Breeding/Nesting Range extends from 11,000 to 13,000 feet

Winter Range extends from 9,500 to 12,300 feet

My ptarmigan—what was the dog doing disturbing my birds? I felt anger rise in my throat. Where were the dog's owners? Why didn't they control their dog?

I skied over and found lots of ptarmigan tracks. Finally I saw three birds huddled next to a krummholz tree. I watched them for a while and skied on. The dog came back toward me, causing two more birds to fly. I tried to catch the dog but it bounded away. Then I heard voices, and skied until I found a couple packing up their camp. They had spent the night in the forest near the willow areas the ptarmigan use during winter.

Controlling my anger, I told the campers I was conducting a survey and asked them how many ptarmigan they had seen.

"What's a ptarmigan?" they asked.

"Did you see any white birds?" I replied.

"Oh, yeah. We didn't know any birds would be here in winter," they answered.

I told the couple about my study and explained to them that their dog in flushing the birds and making them fly was putting undue stress upon the ptarmigan. "These birds are living on the edge," I said. "They stay warm in winter by eating willow buds, which are nutritious, by roosting in the snow, and by walking rather than flying to conserve energy."

The couple, even without my prompting, put their dog on a leash and thanked me. We said our goodbyes. I went on to ski around the lake to look for more birds and they went homeward. I can only hope the couple gained a greater understanding and appreciation for my favorite birds.

Finally, there is a fear that global warming will eventually lead to local extinction of ptarmigan. These birds are efficient at keeping warm in cold climates but are unable to thrive at high temperatures. If alpine areas become too warm, ptarmigan are likely to survive poorly. Since white-tailed ptarmigan are the only avian species that lives in alpine areas year-round, they are ideal indicators of the health of alpine ecosystems.

A look at the distribution of white-tailed ptarmigan in alpine ecosystems throughout the year shows that they utilize different habitats as well as different elevations in the mountains during different seasons. Thus, it is important to preserve the integrity of the entire system for the health of these exceptional birds.

We need to be mindful of our actions that may upset natural balances. We need to keep wild lands wild so the integrity of natural ecosystems continues to flourish. We need to protect alpine areas from disturbances so that white-tailed ptarmigan continue to thrive. All of us need to know wild areas exist both for ourselves and for all parts of nature.

GLOSSARY

Afterfeather. A feather having another feather growing from the base of its main feather axis. This second feather has an extra layer of highly branched downy filaments, increasing its insulative quality.

Alpine. The highest elevational life zone in the mountains. This is a treeless region above timberline, above 11,250 feet in elevation in the Colorado Rocky Mountains.

Barbules. Interlocking hooks that zip the vanes of a feather together to keep it firm.

Breeding territory. An area of ten to eighty acres that a ptarmigan pair use during courtship, mating, and nesting. The male ptarmigan protects the area while his mate builds a nest, lays eggs, and incubates them until the chicks hatch.

Brood. The chicks produced by a hen. The term is also used when a hen insulates and protects eggs or young chicks with her warm body.

Brood patch. An area where a hen plucks feathers from her abdomen, creating a naked vascular patch that allows heat to flow efficiently from the hen to the eggs or chicks.

Bulblets. Roundish vegetative reproductive knots that grow along the plant stalk of viviparous bistort and some other alpine plants, capable of germinating and producing new individuals.

Caecum. A pouch between the small and large intestines where bacteria aid in the digestion of fibrous material (plural: caeca).

Circumpolar. A plant or animal having a distribution in northern latitudes around the world.

Clutch. The eggs laid by the hen; ptarmigan have an average clutch size of six or seven eggs.

Contour feathers. Feathers that cover a bird's body, giving it a streamlined shape.

Crop. A pouch where food is first stored when a bird eats; this leads to the gizzard.

Down feathers. Soft feathers located beneath contour feathers with fluffy filaments and noninterlocking barbs that trap air.

Eye comb. A red-orange stripe above the eye that males flare to attract females. In females the eye comb is smaller than in males, but females sometimes display their eye comb when disturbed.

Form. A depression in the snow where a ptarmigan has spent the night; it is often filled with the bird's scat.

Gizzard. A muscular pouch where small stones aid in grinding food particles into smaller pieces that are further digested in the small intestine.

Grit. Tiny bits of sharp rock that birds ingest to aid in mechanically grinding food into smaller pieces in the gizzard.

Hibernation. Physiological adaptations that slow metabolic processes to a minimum in the winter.

Incubation period. The time a hen sits upon her eggs until the chicks hatch; in ptarmigan the incubation period lasts twenty-two to twenty-four days.

Krummholz. German for "crooked wood." Krummholz describes the distorted shapes of trees between the area of timberline and treelimit; trees are short in stature, distorted in shape, and range from having flagged branches to growing in small mats called "tree islands."

Lee. A sheltered area protected from the wind.

Molting. Changes in the color of feathers as an adaptation to a change of season.

Montane. A mid-elevation forest zone in the mountains, between 8,000 and 9,500 feet in the Colorado Rocky Mountains.

Noose pole. An extendable pole with a loop on the end developed to catch ptarmigan or grouse.

Piloerection. When a bird contracts muscles connected to their feathers to fluff themselves up and increase the air spaces between feathers.

Pip. When a chick first pecks or breaks through an egg; this occurs twenty-four to forty-eight hours before the chick hatches.

Precocial. Chicks that hatch well developed, fully feathered, and with eyes open.

Preen. When birds clean and straighten their feathers to keep them in top shape and free of parasites.

Primary wing feathers. The feathers borne on the hand of a bird's wing; secondaries are on the forearm. The ten primary feathers of ptarmigan remain white in all seasons.

Rachis. The central axis of a feather.

Rectrices. In birds, feathers of the tail.

Renest. When a bird lays a second clutch of eggs after the first ones have been destroyed, either due to environmental extremes or actions of a predator.

Scat. Animal droppings; the waste product of digestion.

Semiplume feather. A feather intermediate between a vaned (contour) feather and a down feather. Semiplumes have a rachis with barbs arranged in two rows as in a vaned feather, but the barbs lack hooks and are loose and fluffy as in a down feather. Typically they occur under a covering of contour feathers.

Subalpine. The life zone lower than the alpine zone; the highest forested zone and dominated by subalpine fir and Engelmann spruce trees. In Colorado this zone ranges between 9,500 and 11,500 feet in elevation.

Timberline. The elevation above which trees do not grow in a continuous forest. Trees are distorted in shape by the wind.

Treelimit. The elevation above which trees, or krummholz, do not grow. Treelimit is the highest reach of trees in any form.

Tundra. The treeless plain of arctic regions or the land above the trees in high mountains.

Vane. The web or flat part of a feather.

Viviparous. A vegetative method of reproduction in plants, such as bulblets on bistort, which can germinate without the union of an egg and a sperm cell.

Windward. The area facing into the wind.

BIBLIOGRAPHY

Artiss, T. A., and K. Martin. 1995. "Male vigilance in white-tailed ptarmigan, *Lagopus leucurus*: mate guarding or predator detection." *Animal Behavior* 49: 1249–1258.

Bradbury, W. C. 1915. "Notes on the nesting of white-tailed ptarmigan in Colorado." *Condor* 17: 214–222.

Braun, C. E., K. Martin, and L. A. Robb. 1993. "White-tailed ptarmigan (*Lagopus leucurus*)." In *The Birds of North America*, A. Poole and F. Gill., eds. No. 68. Philadelphia: The Academy of Natural Sciences; Washington, DC: The American Ornithologists' Union. Contains an extensive bibliography.

Braun, C. E., and G. E. Rogers. 1971. "The white-tailed ptarmigan in Colorado." Technical Publication No. 27, Colorado Division of Game, Fish, and Parks.

———. 1976. "Wintering areas and winter ecology of white-tailed ptarmigan in Colorado." Special Report No. 38, Colorado Division of Wildlife.

Braun, C. E., D. R. Stevens, K. M. Giesen, and C. P. Melcher. 1991. "Elk, white-tailed ptarmigan and willow relationships: A management dilemma in Rocky Mountain National Park." *Transaction of the North American Wildlife and Natural Resources Conference* 56: 74–85.

Cushman, R.C. 1980. "On the Ptrail of the Ptarmigan." *American Forests* (December): 46–51.

Giesen, K. M., and C. E. Braun. 1979a. "Nesting behavior of female white-tailed ptarmigan in Colorado." *Condor* 81: 215–217.

———. 1979b. "Renesting of female white-tailed ptarmigan in Colorado." *Condor* 81: 217–218.

———. 1979c. "A technique for age determination of juvenile white-tailed ptarmigan." *Journal of Wildlife Management* 43: 508–511.

———. 1992. "Winter home range and habitat characteristics of white-tailed ptarmigan in Colorado." *Wilson Bulletin* 104: 263–272.

Hoffman, R. W. 2006. "White-tailed ptarmigan (*Lagopus leucura*): A technical conservation assessment." USDA Forest Service, Rocky Mountain Region. Contains an extensive bibliography. Available online: http://www.fs.fed.us/r2/projects/scp/assessments/whitetailedptarmigan.pdf.

Hoffman, R. W., and C. E. Braun. 1977. "Characteristics of a wintering population of white-tailed ptarmigan in Colorado." *Wilson Bulletin* 89: 107–115.

Larison, J. R., G. E. Likens, J. W. Fitzpatrick, and J. G. Crock. 2000. "Cadmium toxicity among wildlife in the Colorado Rocky Mountains." *Nature* 406: 181–183.

Martin, K., P. B. Stacey, and C. E. Braun. 2000. "Recruitment, dispersal, and demographic rescue in spatially-structured white-tailed ptarmigan populations." *Condor* 102: 503–516.

Martin, K., R. F. Holt, and D. W. Thomas. 1993. "Getting on high: ecological energetics of arctic and alpine grouse." In *Life in the Cold*, C. Carey, G. L. Forant, B. A. Wunder, and B. Horwitz, eds. 34–41. Boulder: Westview Press.

May, T. A., and C. E. Braun. 1972. "Seasonal foods of adult white-tailed ptarmigan in Colorado." *Journal of Wildlife Management* 36: 1180–1186.

Schenk, M., D. Powers, and E. Collette. 2006. "Guanella Pass visitor use and white-tailed ptarmigan research project." Colorado Division of Wildlife.

Schmidt, R. K., Jr. 1969. "Behavior of white-tailed ptarmigan in Colorado." Master of Science thesis. Colorado State University, Fort Collins, Colorado.

Walters, V. 1991. "Ghosts of the Alpine Tundra." *Birder's World* (June): 10–14.

Wang, G., N. T. Hobbs, K. M. Giesen, H. Galbraith, D. S. Ojima, and C. E. Braun. 2002. "Relationship between climate and population dynamics of white-tailed ptarmigan *Lagopus leucurus* in Rocky Mountain National Park, Colorado." *Climate Research* 23: 81–87.

INDEX

JOYCE GELLHORN, a mountain ecologist, cross-country skis from November until June, backpacks from June until October, and travels wherever there are mountains to explore. She is the author of *Song of the Alpine*, which was a finalist for both the Colorado Book Award and the Mountain and Plains Bookseller Association Award.

Joyce holds a Ph.D. in botany from the University of Colorado with a specialty in plant ecology. She has taught biology, botany, ecology, and natural history classes in Colorado, Wyoming, and Alaska for over 30 years, and has been photographing the high country for the same length of time. Presently, she teaches ecology and outdoor education seminars at the University of Colorado's Mountain Research Station, the Gore Range Natural Science School, and the Boulder County Nature Association.

CALVIN WHITEHALL specializes in photographing wildflowers, ptarmigan, and abstracts in nature. He has been the featured artist at the Boulder Barnes and Noble Bookstore and the National Center for Atmospheric Research. He has also been juried into the prestigious Louisville Center for the Arts, the Art Center of Estes Park and the Boulder Art Association

national shows. One of Cal's ptarmigan photographs was judged "Best of Show" in a recent show at the Louisville Center for the Arts.